PSYCHOLOGY

PSYCHOLOGY

FROM SPIRITS TO PSYCHOTHERAPY:
THE MIND THROUGH THE AGES

ANNE ROONEY

This edition published in 2020 by Arcturus Publishing Limited
26/27 Bickels Yard, 151–153 Bermondsey Street,
London SE1 3HA

AD006719UK

Printed in the UK

Contents

INTRODUCTION
The study of humanity

'The proper study of mankind is man.'
Alexander Pope, *Essay on Man* (1732–34)

For more than two thousand years, psychology – the study
of the human mind, its characteristics and thought processes
– was a branch of philosophy. Scholarly interest in the natur
and workings of the human mind is believed to have start
with the Ancient Greeks, though the subject also featu
in Ancient Chinese writings. For thousands of years
mind and soul were not clearly distinguished. The soul

considered to animate the body and be the agent of thought, feeling, creativity and myriad other mental attitudes. This explains why one of the earliest texts to address psychology in its broadest sense was *De Anima* ('On the Soul'), by the Greek philosopher Aristotle (384–322BC).

The science of human nature

In the 18th century, Scottish philosopher David Hume (1711–76) set out to devise a 'science of human nature' which would be as logical and empirical as the physical sciences already set out by astronomer Galileo Galilei (1564–1642) and physicist Isaac Newton (1643–1727). Hume determined that his new science of the mind would be based on the observation of experiences and how they relate to one another. For all his good intentions, Hume didn't institute a science of psychology. The study of psychology in the modern sense began in 1879 when German physician and philosopher Wilhelm Wundt (1832–1920) set up the first psychology laboratory in Leipzig in Germany. Wundt was the first person to describe himself as a 'psychologist'. Today we define psychology as relating to all expressions of the mind, including behaviour and perception; reflex actions and physical needs; the way in which mental and physical states interact; and how psychological adaptations help humans survive and thrive.

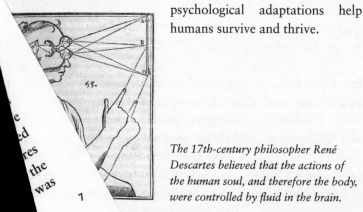

The 17th-century philosopher René Descartes believed that the actions of the human soul, and therefore the body, were controlled by fluid in the brain.

1

SO IS PSYCHOLOGY A SCIENCE?

The traditional definition of science is as an endeavour that begins with empirical observation (something we have noticed about the world) and proceeds through inductive reasoning to explain it and propose rules (construct a theory) which allow us to make predictions. The predictions are tested experimentally: if they are correct, the theory is reinforced; if they are incorrect, the theory must be modified or discarded. At any point, a new observation might overturn the theory.

WELCOME TO THE BRAIN

The earliest example of a word for 'brain' appears in the Edwin Smith papyrus, a medical text written in Egypt around 1500BC. It describes 48 cases of trauma, mostly the result of falls or battle injuries, and advises how to treat them. There are 27 cases relating to head injury, and many of these refer to the brain, the meninges (the membranes surrounding the brain) and cerebrospinal fluid. The convoluted surface of the brain is described as 'like those corrugations which form in molten copper'. The text recognizes the impact of brain and spinal injury on the rest of the body.

In the 20th century, Austro–British philosopher Karl Popper (1902–94) challenged that view, arguing that scientific enquiry should begin with a problem we want to solve and reach a conclusion based on empirical observation. He claimed that a theory must be capable of being proved wrong; in other words, we should be able to predict the results or observations that would prove a theory to be false. For example, suppose we have a theory that all swans are white. This is falsified the moment we find a swan of a different colour.

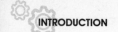

American physicist and philosopher Thomas Kuhn (1922–96) also challenged the traditional model. He believed that science is driven by 'paradigms'. A paradigm is a universally or widely accepted framework, and research takes place within its confines. Occasionally the paradigm is found to be inadequate and a revolutionary change occurs (a 'paradigm shift'). For example, for many centuries astronomy progressed on the basis of the geocentric model, which placed Earth at the centre of the universe, but it became increasingly difficult to fit observations to this paradigm. Copernicus' revolutionary new model, which placed the Sun at the centre, represented a paradigm shift.

Psychology is still a nascent discipline: there is much we don't understand about the working and nature of the mind, and psychologists are still developing and experimenting with new methods of inquiry. There is still no consensus about whether it should be fully considered a science.

TYPES OF PSYCHOLOGY

The history of psychology has been dominated by a series of approaches:

Voluntarism – *the first form of experimental psychology, pioneered by Wilhelm Wundt in Germany in 1879;*

Structuralism – *an approach led by British psychologist Edward Titchener (1867–1927), which attempted to break down mental processes into their smallest indivisible elements;*

Functionalism – *the 'how?' and 'why?' of brain function, first examined by American psychologist William James (1842–1910);*

Psychodynamism – *psychoanalysis, the first psychodynamic therapy, was pioneered by the Austrian neurologist Sigmund*

Freud (1856–1939) in Vienna in the 1890s; it held that neuroses were rooted in repressed experiences and attempted to alleviate them through 'talking therapy';

Gestaltism – Czech-born psychologist Max Wertheimer (1880–1943) visualized mental events 'holistically' (in the context of the whole body);

Behaviourism – beginning with the work of John Broadus Watson (1878–1958) in 1913, behaviourism focused on observable physical behaviours rather than mental processes;

Humanistic psychology – in a reaction against negative and partial approaches to the human mind, humanistic psychology, begun by American psychologist Abraham Maslow (1908–70), examined the whole person and the uniqueness of each individual;

Cognitive psychology – concerned with mental processes such as learning and processing information, which began in the 1950s with the work of George A. Miller (1920–2012) and Ulric Neisser (1928–2012);

Social psychology – the way in which the individual behaves in the presence of others, an approach pioneered in the 1960s and 1970s by Stanley Milgram (1933–84) and Philip Zimbardo (b.1933).

In the late 20th century, some schools of psychology combined with other theoretical approaches, such as neurophysiology, evolutionary biology, computing, linguistics and anthropology.

CHAPTER 1
What and where is the mind?

'For it is the same thing to think and to be.'
Parmenides (born *c.*515BC)

Where and what is the thing we identify as 'I'? The question is as old as culture itself, and central to psychology. Is 'I' just a physical body? If so, what makes one person so very different in character from another? Many people believe that the mind, or perhaps something called the soul, makes us what we are. Some believe that only biochemical processes mark the differences between individuals.

Mind and matter

The way in which humans use language suggests that the mind is not the same as the physical body. Phrases such as 'I felt myself do . . . ' and 'I can't bring myself to . . . ' suggest a split between the mind and body. This 'dualist' position supposes that there are two different entities involved in an individual's makeup. One is the physical matter that makes up flesh and bones; the other is an inspiring spirit, energy, consciousness – or soul.

If the mind and the body are separate, in what way are they related and how do they interact? This question underscores many of the issues discussed in psychology and its therapeutic applications in psychiatry and psychotherapy, and even in other aspects of medicine. Some philosophers take the 'monist' view – that things can be explained in terms of a single reality or substance. The 'materialistic monist' position holds that there is only the physics and chemistry of our bodies, and everything we consider to be a mental event is produced by physical impulses. Radical behaviourist psychologists such as Burrhus Frederick ('B. F.') Skinner (1904–90) held that the mind does not exist; they assert that humans are simply their bodies, and everything they do can be described in terms of behaviour.

The 'idealist monist' position states that human actions are psychological events and the physical counts for nothing at all and might not even exist. A psychologist taking this position explains everything in terms of consciousness and psychological acts. The 18th-century Anglo–Irish philosopher Bishop George Berkeley (1685–1753) was an idealist monist: he claimed that the external world doesn't exist except insofar as it is perceived by human consciousness.

In Ancient Greece, before the time of Socrates, the soul was seen as something which distinguished a living person from a corpse. It was the 'spirit of life' and that was its only role – it wasn't held responsible for behaviour, thought, emotions, intellect or any of the other attributes of the mind. Initially only humans were believed to have a soul. The soul didn't go anywhere after death or have any supernatural connotations; it was simply the state of a living person to be 'ensouled' and of a dead person to be lacking one. Slowly, the meaning of 'soul' changed and it came to be applied to any living thing. In the 5th century BC, it was associated with virtues such as courage, and with some actions of the mind – principally, higher motives such as a love of learning. The Greek philosopher Socrates (c.470–399BC) believed that the body was responsible for desires, fears, beliefs and pleasures. The soul was responsible for keeping the body in check and policing its baser instincts. In this sense, it served much the same purpose as the faculty of reason.

Three in one

Plato (c.425–c.348BC) proposed a three-part soul. The 'appetitive' soul is concerned with satisfying physical appetites – the body's desire for food, drink, sex, sensation. The 'courageous' soul is

Plato's allegory of the charioteer steering two horses explains the idea of the three-part soul.

concerned with the emotions – love, hate, fear, courage and so on. The 'rational' soul seeks knowledge and keeps the other two parts in check, with varying degrees of success. In *Phaedo*, Plato uses the allegory of the charioteer to explain the relationship between the three aspects of the soul. The charioteer is the rational soul trying to steer his carriage pulled by two horses, one black and one white. The black horse is the appetitive soul, and the white horse is the courageous soul. The black horse is trying to pull the chariot towards fine dinners and whore-houses while the white horse is pulling in the direction of acts of valour and benevolence. The charioteer tries to control the two vying parts of the soul and tries to negotiate the best course of action.

> *'What is it that, when present in a body, makes it living? —*
> *A soul.'*
>
> Plato's *Phaedo* ('On the Soul')

Plato's pupil Aristotle (384–322BC) proposed a different trio of souls. He believed that each animate thing, from plant to human being, has a soul suited to its function, with capabilities and duties appropriate to the organism. This might include abilities such as growth (in a plant), locomotion (in an animal) and abstract reasoning (in a human). With this theory, Aristotle touched on concepts regarding the function of the brain which we consider to be exclusively modern. The brain does regulate voluntary and involuntary activities such as breathing and moving; but it is also the site of non-physical activities such as contemplation, desire and reasoning. Unlike Plato, Aristotle didn't believe that the soul could survive the body or have any existence independent of it. In this, too, the Aristotelian soul is closer to the modern concept of 'mind' than that of a semi-mystical spirit.

In two minds

In Epicurean tradition, based on the teachings of the Ancient Greek philosopher Epicurus (341–270BC), the soul has two parts – one rational, and the other non-rational. The rational part, called *animus* (mind), produces emotions and impulses, applies concepts, shapes beliefs, assesses evidence, interprets sensory perceptions, and so on. The non-rational part receives sense-impressions – sights, sounds, smells and so on. (Any errors arise later on, when the rational part of the soul is interpreting these stimuli.) The non-rational part also transmits impulses which originate in the rational part, and carries out non-reasoning tasks such as seeing and breathing. These practical tasks carried out by the brain are also achieved by animals we would not always assume to have a soul or conscious thought processes, such as hedgehogs and prawns.

HEART AND SOUL

While it's obvious to us that the brain is the part of the body that does the thinking, feeling, dreaming, believing and so on, until recently there was no anatomical evidence for this and earlier generations didn't necessarily consider it as the locus for thought. The Ancient Egyptians believed the heart was the centre of emotions, reason and thought. They discarded the brain when they mummified their dead, even though they carefully preserved all the other organs in Coptic jars for burial. Plato suggested that the brain was the site of thought, but Aristotle rejected this idea, plumping for the heart once again.

The Stoics (see panel opposite) took the crucial step towards suggesting something like the prevailing modern view of the mind. They believed there were three types of *pneuma*, or inspiring spirit (*pneuma* means 'breath'). The first was thought to hold solid matter together and was present even in rocks; today we would ascribe this to the laws of physics and the behaviour of atoms and molecules. The second was believed to provide the vital functions of plant life (growth, respiration and so on). The third, the soul, was thought to provide the mental and psychological functions of animals and humans. It varied in its capabilities according to the animal, so in a human included reason, belief, intellect and desire as well as basic mental processes such as sensory perception.

The Stoic conception of the soul is not as an animating spirit, the breath of life, or the difference between being alive or dead. It's a conglomeration of mental processes that provide awareness, understanding, thought, consciousness and meaningful inter-action with the world.

THE STOICS
Stoicism was a school of philosophy started by Zeno of Citium (334–262BC) in Athens in the early 3rd century BC. The Stoics thought that destructive emotions such as hatred and envy occur through errors of judgement, and maintained that only a wise man can be truly happy. Later Stoics included the Roman philosopher Seneca the Younger (4BC–AD65) and the Greek sage, Epictetus (c.AD55–135).

Soul-grabbers

With the rise of monotheistic religions, the soul was hijacked in the service of God and became a shard of divinity resident in each human body, reflecting or struggling towards a godhead.

The Neoplatonists, such as the Jewish philosopher Philo of Alexandria (*c.*25BC–AD50) and the Roman thinker Plotinus (204–270), adopted the mystical aspects of Plato's thinking and adapted it to religion. Philo melded Plato's division between sensory and rational aspects of the human with Hebrew religious teaching, taking as his starting point the Jewish model of the physical body imbued with a soul that is a fragment of the divine being. Unlike Plato, he didn't believe that introspection and reason would lead to knowledge; he thought that wisdom could come only from God, by divine inspiration. To prepare the soul for the gift of knowledge, Philo considered it necessary to eschew bodily impulses by way of meditation and distancing oneself from base appetites. He believed that inspiration could also strike in dreams and trances, as these distance the soul from the physical world. Plotinus thought the soul reflected the spirit, which was itself an image of 'the One'. This gave a three-part hierarchy, with the One at the top, imperfectly imaged in the spirit, and the spirit imperfectly imaged in the Soul. He taught that, in entering a body, the spirit merged with something inferior.

The Platonic and Neoplatonic model of the soul struggling to master the bodily impulses appealed to Christian theology. It required only a minor reworking to have the noble soul striving towards godliness while the imperfect body tries to drag it down to frolic in wayward pleasures. This tweaking was accomplished by the early Christian philosopher Augustine of Hippo (345–430). Eight hundred years later, the Italian priest Thomas Aquinas (1225–74) did the same tweaking and accommodation for Aristotelian theory. In the main, though, the period following the fall of the Roman Empire was a fruitless one for the development of psychological thought in Europe. The soul/mind was in thrall to God and any interpretation of its workings was therefore theological. Instead it was the Arab world that kept the flame of learning alive.

In the footsteps of the prophet

After the death of Mohamet in 632, Islam spread rapidly throughout the Arab and Persian world. Middle Eastern thinkers read the works of the Ancient Greeks, particularly Aristotle, and wrote translations and commentaries on them, and Aristotle's writings resurfaced in Europe in the Middle Ages. For a period of around 400 years, Middle Eastern culture made great strides in all branches of science – until Islam took a more intellectually conservative, curiosity-stifling turn in the 12th century.

One of the most important Islamic scholars was the 11th-century Persian polymath Ibn Sina, known as Avicenna in the West. His work was firmly rooted in Aristotle. In psychology, Ibn Sina is most famous for his 'floating man' thought experiment. Imagine you have suddenly been created, from nothing, suspended in mid-air and without any sensory input from the environment or a body. Ibn Sina claimed that because it is possible to conceive of this existence and to be thinking and conscious in this state and not doubt one's existence, it is clear that the mind is a real entity separate from the body:

> *'Therefore the nafs [self, soul], whose existence the person has affirmed, is [his/her] characteristic identity that is not identical to the body nor the limbs . . . [Therefore] the affirmation of the existence of its-self (soul, al-nafs) is distinct from the body and something that is quite non-body.'*

Ibn Sina required the soul to have sufficient connection with the body to be individual (not just a fragment of a universal soul), but sufficiently separate from it to survive bodily death. He followed the Greek physician and philosopher Galen of Pergamon (AD130–200) in believing that parts of the soul were localized in different organs of the body:

> *'In general, there are four types of proper spirit: One is brutal spirit, residing in the heart and it is the origin of*

all spirits. Another – as physicians refer to it – is sensual spirit, residing in the brain. The third – as physicians refer to it – is natural spirit, residing in the liver. The fourth is generative [or procreative] spirit, residing in the gonads. These four spirits go between the soul of absolute purity and the body of absolute impurity.'

Ibn Sina, *Canon of Medicine* (1025)

The internal drama of good and evil

While the Arab world was developing Aristotle's ideas, his theories were lost to most of Europe until the 12th century. Even after they became available to Europeans again, it made little difference to the average person. The struggle inside each person's mind and soul between the impulses to behave well or to follow the body's natural base urges remained essentially religious. On the one hand, the soul would strive towards God; on the other, the body was drawn towards physical pleasures. This struggle had been addressed by Aristotle more than 1,500 years previously, but it was now cloaked in religious language.

OF THE TWO SPIRITS

'God created man to rule the world, and appointed for him two spirits after whose direction he was to walk until the final Inquisition. They are the spirits of truth and perversity.

'The origin of truth lies in the Fountain of Light, and that of perversity in the Wellspring of Darkness. All who practise righteousness are under the domination of the Prince of Lights, and walk in ways of light; whereas all who practise perversity are under the domination of the Angel of

Darkness, however, even those who practise righteousness are made liable to error. All their sin and their iniquities, all their guilt and their deeds of transgression are the result of his domination . . .

'It is to these things that all men are born, and it is to these that all the host of them are heirs throughout their generations. It is in these ways that men needs must walk and it is in these two divisions, according as a man inherits something of each, that all human acts are divided throughout all the ages of eternity.'

From the *Manual of Discipline*, the Dead Sea Scrolls

Freeing the spirit

With the flowering of creativity that came with the Renaissance in the 14th century, Europe finally set out again on the path of intellectual endeavour. Although people were still not free to think whatever they liked – there were plenty of heretics being burned – there was certainly more freedom for exploration and expression as long as it was couched in ways the Church didn't regard as too provocative.

IBN SINA (AVICENNA) (980–1037)
A child prodigy, Ibn Sina had memorized the entire Koran by the time he was ten and was a physician by the age of 20. His expertise extended to many disciplines and he wrote nearly 450 books, of which around 240 survive. Forty of his works are on medicine, including aspects of mental health and the nature of the mind. His 14-volume Canon of Medicine *was used in some European universities until*

> 1650; *that's the equivalent of a modern university using a text book written around the time of the Black Death.*

As science was able to progress once more, it became more objective. Physical laws had been discovered that explained the path of an arrow or a cannonball and even the motion of the planets (around the Sun, now, not around the Earth). The prevailing view was that mathematical and scientific laws lay behind all natural phenomena and could be discovered through observation and reason. The notion that the world – indeed, the universe – was explicable was revolutionary. And if the movement of the planets or the path of a cannonball was susceptible to investigation and explanation, why not ourselves?

THE ENLIGHTENMENT

The Enlightenment was a cultural movement which promoted rational thought and empirical science, denounced superstitious beliefs and sought to challenge traditional ideas, rejecting them if they did not stand up to rigorous scrutiny. It started in 17th-century Europe – particularly England and France – and its key figures included the scientists Francis Bacon (1561–1626) and Isaac Newton (1643–1727), and the philosophers René Descartes, Baruch Spinoza and David Hume. The movement was closely tied to the Scientific Revolution, and marked the beginning of the modern period.

One or two?

French mathematician and philosopher René Descartes (1596–1650) was greatly influenced by the mechanistic approach to science and the world of the Enlightenment. Descartes developed Cartesian geometry as a way of demonstrating the mathematical relationships between objects in three-dimensional space. In 1628, English physician William Harvey (1578–1657) had explained the movement of blood through the body – implying that even the body was a type of machine. Descartes seized on this notion – but what then was the soul, or the mind?

Descartes concluded that although the body is a material object controlled by mechanistic laws, the spirit is immaterial. He assigned as much mental activity as possible to the body. So perception, memory, imagination and common sense were all explained in terms of the sensory organs and nerves. What was left – the uniquely human – was self-awareness and language, and these were the functions of the spirit.

I DOUBT, THEREFORE I AM

Descartes sought to base his philosophical enquiries in some certainty. He discovered that the only thing he could be sure of

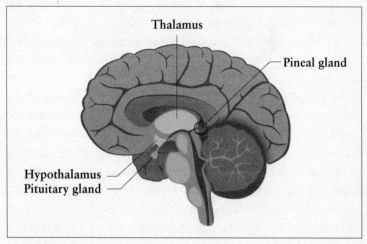

Descartes believed that the soul resides in the pineal gland, once described as the 'third eye', deep in the centre of the brain.

was his own existence, leading to his famous dictum *cogito ergo sum* ('I think, therefore I am'). He arrived at this by realizing that all he saw or experienced might be no more real than a dream; but his existence was proven by the fact that he doubted the veracity of his perception and thought about the issue. This recalls Ibn Sina's 'floating man' thought experiment around 600 years previously.

As later critics pointed out, Descartes hadn't really proved his own existence. He had proved the existence of thought, but not that he was doing the thinking or existed *because* he was doing it. But his argument established a distinction between the physical and spiritual/psychological identities.

The notion that thinking could take place without any sensory input from the body suggested a degree of separation between mind (or soul) and body. Descartes developed a model of body/soul dualism that, much later, British philosopher Gilbert Ryle (1900–76) called the 'ghost in the machine' (see page 31). Still, the spirit had to be somewhere.

Descartes decided that it resides in the pineal gland, deep within the brain. But if the soul was immaterial, how could it *be* anywhere? How could it have an effect on the material body, and how could it be affected by it? It was clear to Descartes that there is an influence, in both directions, for an injury to the body (or bodily pleasure) has an effect on the mind; and moods of the mind are expressed through the body. This can happen in quite extreme ways: the physical manifestations of mental distress can look like bodily illness, such as trembling, nausea and pain in the stomach or head. Descartes was unusual for his time in considering there to be two-way traffic between body and soul. But he couldn't answer the question of how the immaterial soul and the material body could interact. It is a question that remains unanswered today.

'It is one and the same man who is conscious, both that he understands and that he senses. But one cannot sense without a body, and therefore the body must be some part of man.'

Thomas Aquinas, *Summa Theologiae* (1265–74)

Gottfried Leibniz (see panel on pages 27–8) tackled the issue of how the mind/soul and body interact by asserting that they didn't need to. Leibniz said that both entities follow independent deterministic paths and move forward in parallel. God set them running and, like two clocks started together that keep perfect time, they will always be synchronized. Consequently, mental states and acts are always in accord with bodily sensations and actions.

THE SEAT OF THE SOUL

Descartes had two reasons for supposing that the soul resided in the pineal gland. At the time it was considered to be one of the few parts of the brain which didn't come in pairs (although it is now known to have two hemispheres). Therefore, as we can only have one soul, and there is only one pineal gland, Descartes teamed them up. The pineal gland is located near the ventricles of the brain, which contain cerebrospinal fluid. Descartes believed that the body was controlled by the cerebrospinal fluid affecting the nerves; he thought sensations were carried from the nerves through the cerebrospinal fluid to the pineal gland, and would make it vibrate, producing emotions. The body's actions were the result of outgoing messages sent from the pineal gland, so it

> *was the perfect seat of command for the soul. Interestingly, several mystical traditions hold the pineal gland to be the 'third eye', important in spiritual experience.*

The mechanism of the mind

Although Descartes saw the human body as mechanistic, he believed the soul or mind to be of a different substance. English philosopher Thomas Hobbes (1588–1679) and French priest and mathematician Pierre Gassendi (1592–1655) both went a step further in their adoption of the mechanistic model.

Contrary to Descartes, Gassendi didn't see why the body should obey physical rules and not the mind. He didn't distinguish between the mind and the brain, but adopted a position of physical (or material) monism – asserting that there is only one type of 'stuff', which is matter. He suspected that Descartes also believed this but was afraid to say so because the Church would have disapproved of such a pronouncement.

Hobbes was a materialist; he saw nothing in the universe besides corporeal matter, which he believed was governed by the mechanistic laws of nature. He considered metaphysics to be bunkum and contended that human actions, like those of animals, are entirely determined by natural laws, which must apply to behaviour and thought as well as to obviously physical activities such as walking and breathing. He held that thought, ideas and knowledge are constructed by the stuff of sensory experience.

'Material monism' dispenses with the problem posed for dualists such as Descartes of how an immaterial spirit can interact with a material body. If both mind and body are made of matter, there is no distinction between them, so there is no communication problem.

'The exploration of the globe having resulted in discoveries that have destroyed many of the data on which ancient philosophy reposed, a new conception of things will inevitably be called for.'

Tommaso Campanella (1568–1639),
Italian friar and philosopher

IT'S ALL ONE

The Dutch–Jewish philosopher Baruch Spinoza (1632–77) also believed that there was no special spiritual substance to the mind. He denied that God was a special being and he was, as a result, excluded from the Jewish faith and reviled by Christians.

MONADS

German philosopher Gottfried Leibniz (1646–1716) had an original view of the world. He believed the universe was composed of an infinite quantity of tiny points or life-units which he called 'monads'. These were present in all matter, including inert matter. Every monad was to some degree alive and conscious. The quality of monads improved as we moved up the hierarchy of living matter from microbes to humans (and even to God). Leibniz thought humans contained some high-quality human-soul monads, together with a mix of lower-order monads, so their thinking

Gottfried Leibniz

> *was not always lucid or accurate. Inert matter and microbes contained very low-grade monads, so weren't capable of much thought. Even the high-quality monads had ideas only in the form of potentialities, which experience or sensory perception could cause to be actualized.*

Spinoza didn't consider the human mind to be separate from the body, but believed them to be aspects of a single substance. This position, called 'neutral monism', saw the whole of the universe consisting of the same substance which manifested in many different modes or modifications. Thus, the whole of nature, which was also equivalent to God, partook of consciousness. This pantheistic/panpsychic position was a neat solution to how mind and body can communicate: although they look different, they are in fact two sides of the same coin.

ANOTHER MONIST OPTION

Clearly, if mind/body dualism posits two types of stuff, material monism says there is only physical matter, and neutral monism contends that both are the same substance, then there is space for another type of monism which argues that there is only spiritual or mental 'stuff'. This latter position was espoused by philosophers such as Bishop George Berkeley. Immaterialism, or subjective idealism, argues that material reality is created by the observer and without an observer has no meaning.

By the mid-18th century, the main positions regarding the body and mind had been established: they are two different types of stuff (with communication problems); they are both the same physical stuff; they are both the same immaterial stuff; they are both different aspects of the same, global, stuff.

'[The universe] is corporeal, that is to say, body. . . .
Also every part of body, is likewise body, and . . .
consequently every part of the universe is body, and that
which is not body, is no part of the universe; and because
the universe is all, that which is no part of it is nothing;
and consequently nowhere.'

Thomas Hobbes (1651)

The consequences of mechanistic models

Spinoza took a deterministic view. In his model, everything happens
according to the immutable laws that govern the universe, and
this includes human thought and actions. Determinism means that
there is no such thing as free will, even though humans believe they
are acting freely. Instead, 'Men are conscious of their desire and
unaware of the causes by which [those desires] are determined.'
All mechanistic models tend towards determinism, for if the body
and mind follow natural laws, all that happens is linked in an
unbroken chain of inevitable consequences through time.

There is a serious consequence, however. If all mental events
and activity are determined and we have no freedom, how can we
hold a person responsible for their actions? Spinoza recognized
this and saw that words such as 'blame' and 'praise' were entirely
inappropriate, as everyone does what he or she is predestined
to do. The only freedom that exists is the freedom to see we
are constrained and understand why we act as we do. Spinoza
postulated that moral concepts such as good and evil must have
their basis in psychology. Many later psychologists, especially
materialists and behaviourists, also believed we don't really have
free will, but for different reasons. With any model that has our
actions determined by past experiences or innate compulsions,

there is the removal (or, at best, the compromise) of free will and responsibility.

THE MECHANISTIC MIND AS COMPUTER

The problem of responsibility and free will troubled French mathematician Blaise Pascal (1623–62). He believed that the mind was similar to a machine such as a computer (Pascal invented an early mechanical calculator), and capable of incredibly complex calculations and operations, but ultimately reducible to logic and laws of information processing. One consequence of this view was that it rendered the human mind no different from the mind of an animal, a conclusion Pascal wasn't happy with. To avoid this, he sought to make free will, instead of reason, the distinguishing feature of humanity. Unfortunately, his account of free will wasn't compatible with his belief in the efficacy of God's grace, so he was left with a situation in which people were either saved or damned according to God's will – so they weren't very free after all.

The model of the mind as a kind of information-processing machine became very popular in the 1960s, with the rise of computing. It was a major concern of cognitive science, which combines elements of computer science (particularly artificial intelligence or AI), linguistics, psychology, neurology, anthropology, philosophy and any other discipline that can yield useful methods or insights.

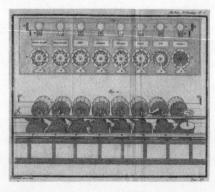

Pascal's early mechanical computer

Cognitive science is concerned with the nature of – and working cognitive processes in – human and animal minds and computers, and explores how information is represented to the mind (perceived), processed (understood and stored) and transformed (in, for example, recall and creative acts).

> 'The infant believes that it is by free will that it seeks the breast; the angry boy believes that by free will he wishes vengeance; the timid man thinks it is with free will he seeks flight; the drunkard believes that by a free command of his mind he speaks the things which when sober he wishes he had left unsaid. . . . All believe that they speak by a free command of the mind, whilst, in truth, they have no power to restrain the impulse which they have to speak.'
>
> **Baruch Spinoza (1677)**

NO DIFFERENCE?

American philosopher Daniel Dennett (b.1942) believes all mental functions and activities are entirely the result of the physiology of the brain, and goes so far as to say that there is no difference between a human mind and the 'mind' of a supremely sophisticated computer. He claims that if we can make a computer which appears to be as intelligent as a human, then it actually *is* as intelligent as a human. There is no meaningful distinction between human and machine intelligence – we are very much a machine with no ghost.

GHOSTS AND SEPARATE STATES

The phrase 'ghost in the machine' was coined in 1949 by British philosopher Gilbert Ryle (1900–76). Rejecting what he saw as the dogma of Descartes' dualistic view of the mind and body (see page 24), Ryle used the phrase disparagingly to describe the idea of a mind or soul (ghost) in a mechanistic body (machine). He regarded this distinction between mind and body as a 'category error', which reduced mental reality to the same status as physical reality.

THE EMERGENCE OF NEUROLOGY
Thomas Willis (1621–75) was an English anatomist and founding member of the Royal Society. His view of the mind/body issue was firmly rooted in what he had learned from dissections and neurological studies, which led him to conclusions that are now widespread in neuropsychiatry and philosophy of mind. In the model Willis described, every psychological aspect of the mind 'supervenes' (depends) on an equivalent neurological aspect. So each mental state or act occurs as a particular firing or connection of neurons in the brain, or a particular chemical response. The mind is not a separate entity, but a product of the neurological workings of the brain. This view is remarkably similar to the one held today by American philosopher John Searle (b.1932) – that consciousness is an emergent property of neurons.

No such thing as mind

The 18th-century Scottish philosopher David Hume (1711–76) agreed with Berkeley that we can never experience the physical world directly, but only as mediated through our senses. He didn't deny the existence of the physical world, but said we have to take it on trust as we have no way of testing reality. Hume went on to say that there is no such thing as the mind, just the sum of our personal experiences and the links we have made with them: 'We may observe, that what we call a mind, is nothing but a heap or collection of different perceptions, united together by certain relations, and suppos'd, tho' falsely, to be endow'd with a perfect simplicity and identity.'

Hume maintained that not only is there no such thing as the mind – just a bundle of perceptions – but there is also no such thing as the 'self', separated from those perceptions. Hume's ideas would become extremely influential in subsequent centuries, as perception came to be recognized as the interface between the world, the body and the mind, and as behaviourists also rejected the idea of a mind 'endow'd with . . . identity'. Hume observed, 'I can never catch myself at any time without a perception' and that when perceptions were removed by sleep he was 'insensible of myself, and may truly be said not to exist'. On death, when his perceptions all ended, he declared that he 'should be entirely annihilated'.

The tri-partite ghost revisited

A hundred years after Hume tried to dismantle the mind, German neurologist Sigmund Freud, founder of psychoanalysis, brought it roaring back. His theory looks remarkably like Plato's charioteer reining in two wayward horses.

Freud identified three parts of the psyche: the 'id', the 'ego' and the 'superego'. The 'id' is the most primitive, need-driven part and its energy, the 'libido', provides the impetus to satisfy needs immediately. The 'ego' is the voice of practical realism. It recognizes the drives of the id and tries to negotiate them, satisfying them as far as possible within the limitations of the physical world. The id acting alone would cause you to snatch a sandwich from a person in the street to satisfy hunger. The ego realizes that such behaviour is likely to get you into trouble – you might get punched or arrested – and sends you to buy your own sandwich.

The superego adds morality to the mix. So instead of not stealing a sandwich because of the consequences, you learn not to do it because it is wrong. Without a superego, a human is much like any other animal (assuming animals don't have an idea of morality). The ego has to negotiate three ways, between the drives of the id, the realities of the external world, and the value-led demands of the superego.

While the id and ego are innate, the superego is present in potential form in the baby, and populated with values through the socialization of the growing child. As a child is rewarded for 'approved' behaviour and punished for 'unapproved' behaviour, the superego builds an internalized set of values. Successful socializing means the individual will feel good if they do or even think about doing approved behaviours and will feel bad (guilty, ashamed, embarrassed, etc.) if they contemplate or carry out unapproved behaviours.

There is inevitably tension between the id, ego and super-ego because of their different goals. Sometimes the ego uses repression as a coping mechanism. If the id's desire is going to cause problems if satisfied or lead to anxiety if contemplated, it might be excluded (repressed) by the conscious mind. Freud believed that the repression of desires or memories was at the root of all neuroses, because the mind sidesteps issues that can't be confronted or acknowledged.

SIGMUND FREUD (1856–1939)
Sigmund Freud was born in Příbor, Moravia (now in the Czech Republic) to poor Jewish parents. He was born with a caul – covered by the amniotic membrane that forms the

sac in which the foetus develops. His mother took this to be a good omen.

He studied medicine at the University of Vienna, then carried out research at the General Hospital there. In 1885 he became a lecturer in neuropathology and went to Paris to study with Jean-Martin Charcot (1825–93), a neurologist researching hypnosis. It was a turning point in Freud's life. The following year, he went into private practice, initially using hypnosis to get his patients to open up and reveal past traumatic experiences.

Freud soon realized he could forgo hypnosis and he developed the technique of 'free association', which allowed his patients to talk about whatever they wished. He began analysing dreams, which gave him an insight into his patients' unconscious minds. He saw all dreams as wish-fulfilment, subject to some censorship, but revealing our inner nature and most secret longings.

As Freud began to publish his theories and case studies, he developed a following. A group of disciples met with him once a week; calling themselves 'the Wednesday Psychological Society', they marked the beginning of the psychoanalytic movement. The Austrian music critic Max Graf (1873–1958), an early member of the group, recalled that, 'there was the atmosphere of the foundation of a religion in that room. Freud himself was its new prophet.'

But Freud was a Jew living in Vienna and, for all his fame and prominence, he felt increasingly threatened after the Nazis' rise to power in Germany in 1933. At a public bonfire of his writings, he commented, 'What progress we are making. In the Middle Ages they would have burned me. Now, they are content with burning my books.' He was finally persuaded (and helped) to leave Austria in 1939, fleeing to London where he died the same year of cancer of the jaw – or, rather, of the overdose of morphine he asked his friend and physician Max Schur to administer.

ME, MYSELF AND I

On the other side of the Atlantic, the pioneer of American psychology, William James (1842–1910), was setting out his theory of the self, initially divided into two – 'Me' and 'I'. The 'Me' self was then subdivided into a further three parts: the material, social and spiritual 'Me'.

The material self comprised the things belonging to the self (or that the self belongs to), and included family, body, clothes and possessions. The social self was the person in relation to others, in any number of social roles. Each of us has many social selves, as we act differently in different social contexts – at work, with family members, with friends, and so on. The spiritual self is our core self, made up of our core values, beliefs, conscience and personality. It is the most fixed of the three, varying little during adult life.

James defined a person's 'Me' self as 'not only his body and his psychic powers, but his clothes and his house, his wife and children, his ancestors and friends, his reputation and works, his lands and horses, and yacht and bank-account' (1890). In claiming as 'mine' not only external objects but even other people ('my mother', even 'my enemy') he produced a diffuse, extended self which leaks into the environment – very much the opposite of the enclosed self of René Descartes, distinct not just from others but even from its own body.

The 'I' self, which is pure ego, is the stream of consciousness that provides an unbroken thread from the past through the present to the future. It also provides a sense of distinctness (contrasting with the appropriating 'Me' self) and of volition – it is responsible for choosing which thoughts to attend to and which to reject, so processing experience. The 'I' self is what we might think of as the mind or soul and, according to James, is not substance and so not susceptible to scientific examination.

WEIGHING THE GHOST

In 1907, American physician Duncan MacDougall (1866–1920) decided to measure the weight of the human soul. He devised a special bed that served also as a scale so that he could monitor the weight of his patients. He then selected six terminally ill patients who were about to die. He made sure each one spent their last days in his weighing-bed and recorded their weight at regular intervals, up to and including the moment of death. From his data he calculated the weight of the soul to be 21 grams – the average weight loss of four of his patients at the point of death. It has since been shown that sloppy science accounted for the results – we still don't know whether there is a soul and, if there is, whether it has any mass.

Ghost gone again

Throughout much of the 20th century, psychology was dominated by a movement called behaviourism. This placed all its emphasis on behaviour that could be observed. Most behaviourists were physical monists, paying attention only to the body; some conceded that the mind might exist, but they had no way of accessing it and its processes directly so felt that it might as well not exist at all.

We still can't locate or define consciousness, and the work of psychologists over the last 150 years has not brought consensus on the nature of the mind/body any closer. By the late 18th century, all the intellectual groundwork for psychology had been laid and the full spectrum of models for how the mind and body might be divided or united was pretty much in place.

THE MIND TRICKING THE BODY

The placebo and nocebo effects show just how difficult it can be to disentangle mind and body. The first is healing apparently produced by a placebo – a treatment with no genuine physiological effect, such as a sugar pill, but which the patient believes to be efficacious. The second is the opposite – an ill effect produced by something harmless. A particularly striking instance of the nocebo effect was reported in 2007: a young man took an overdose of a medicine he was receiving in a clinical trial, believing it to be an antidepressant. He suffered serious physical effects until told that he had been part of the control group and was receiving – and had overdosed on – a harmless placebo. At that point, his symptoms rapidly disappeared. The nocebo effect is also behind the phenomenon of people falling ill and even dying when they know they have been the subject of a curse, and the efficacy of the Australian Aboriginal execution method of 'pointing the bone'.

CHAPTER 2
Measuring the mind

'How can one build up a science upon elements which, by very definition, are said to be private and noncommunicable?'
American psychologist Edward Tolman (1922)

Thinking, feeling, knowing, reasoning, learning, remembering, imagining – as objects of study, all these activities of the mind present unique problems to those who want to study them. They are individual and internal, so are not susceptible to direct measurement or sharing. Even to study your own mind involves a tricksy recursiveness, for it is the mind studying itself. As Hume said, 'I can never catch myself at any time without a perception.' So how can the mind study itself? Bringing the methods of science and reason to bear on such a slippery subject has been an enduring challenge for psychologists.

So – is psychology a science?

These very particular difficulties have led some thinkers to claim that psychology can never be a 'proper' science. The German philosopher Immanuel Kant (1724–1804) doubted there could ever be a 'science of the human mind' because its subject matter was subjective, internal, personal and incapable of external observation, testing or interrogation. A century later, the French positivist August Comte (1798–1857) rejected all knowledge except the publicly shareable observations of scientific enquiry. This meant that any kind of introspection was excluded since it could not be shared for verification. And this meant that psychology was impossible: 'In order to observe, your intellect must pause from activity; yet it is this very activity you want to observe. If you cannot effect the pause you cannot observe; if you do effect it, there is nothing to observe. The results of such a method are in proportion to its absurdity. After 2,000 years of psychological pursuit, no one proposition is established to the satisfaction of its followers. They are divided, to this day, into a multitude of schools, still disputing about the very elements of their doctrine. . . . We ask in vain for any one discovery, great or small, which has been made under this method.'

POPPER TAKES A POP AT PSYCHOLOGY

When Karl Popper became uncomfortable with the prevailing definition of science, he compared the theories of the physicist Albert Einstein with those of two psychologists, Sigmund

Freud and his Austrian contemporary Alfred Adler (1870–1937). Popper realized the significant difference was that Einstein's theory of relativity could be proved wrong by certain observations, while Freud and Adler could interpret any new case according to their own psychodynamic theories. The two psychologists framed all new cases in a way that fitted, and supported, their theories.

To qualify as scientific, a theory must be capable of stating the observations which would cause it to be thrown out. For instance, Isaac Newton's theory of the movement of planetary bodies would have to be thrown out if we found a planet that followed a perfectly square path around its sun. How can Freud's theory of psychoanalysis be proved wrong? It can't – so it's not a scientific theory:

> 'A theory which is not refutable by any conceivable event is non-scientific. Irrefutability is not a virtue of a theory (as people often think), but a vice.'

With developments in other sciences, however, it did become possible to measure and observe some aspects of mental activity. Psychology emerged as the 'science of the human mind' that Kant doubted could exist, its quest to find definitive answers to questions about the human brain.

SEMI-SCIENTIFIC

Some aspects of psychology appear to be scientific, while others are not. In earlier times, certain theories – which parts of the brain are used in different mental activities, for example – could never be tested, but they can now be examined using scientific methods such as brain scans. Other theories – such as whether trauma in childhood might be responsible for criminal or neurotic behaviour in adulthood – still cannot be tested rigorously.

Ways of looking

People have thought about the activities of the mind for thousands of years. The first type of critical thinking was philosophical enquiry, which continues to this day. Philosophy is a rigorous discipline that progresses through logic and structured argument to propose, refute, modify or endorse theories. It can tackle any subject and requires no tools apart from a brain and language. However, it is not a science; the matter of philosophy is not susceptible either to empirical proof or, more importantly in Popper's view, to falsification.

In the 16th century, as anatomists began to discover more about the human body and the ways in which it works, some scientists started to investigate the brain and the nervous system. Physiology, the study of bodily systems, offered a new approach to the mind and its interaction with the body, and one that provided new information and ideas.

A paradigm shift occurred in the mid-19th century when the English naturalist Charles Darwin (1809–82) proposed the theory of 'evolution by natural selection' in his seminal work *On the Origin of Species* (1859). This book changed the way people thought about humanity's place in the world and challenged preconceived notions about science and knowledge. According to Darwin, the distinction between humans and animals was no longer clear-cut: the differential was now between humans and *other* animals, and this made a lot of people very uncomfortable. However, it also meant that if humans and animals were not so very different, perhaps useful information could be gathered from studying animal cognition and development. This made studies in comparative psychology – psychological experiments on animals – a potentially useful tool in the exploration of the human mind. At much the same time, advances in technology meant that some mental processes could be measured, observed and recorded. Psychology emerged as a discrete discipline and psychologists began to approach the mind through experimentation. Twenty years after the publication of *On the Origin of Species*, the first laboratory for experimental psychology was opened.

Child-as-guinea-pig

According to the Greek historian Herodotus (*c*.484–425BC), Psamtik I reigned as king of Egypt from 664–610BC. He has been credited with the first experiment in psychology. In order to discover whether humans have an innate capacity for speech, he ordered two newborn babies to be given to a shepherd to care for, with strict instructions that no one should ever speak to them, or talk in their hearing. Psamtik hoped that the babies would begin talking by using an innate knowledge of language. After two years, the babies began to speak and the word they used most often was 'bèkos', which is the Phrygian word for bread. Psamtik took this as proof that humans have an innate capacity for language and that the Phrygian language was the language we were born to speak.

THE FORBIDDEN EXPERIMENT

The idea of raising children without language or any form of human contact has been named the 'forbidden experiment' as it is clearly highly unethical (and inhumane); nevertheless, its potential as a scientific tool is considerable. It has reportedly been tried on several occasions.

In the 13th century, the Holy Roman Emperor Frederick II had infants raised without hearing human speech. The experiment was reported by the Italian friar and chronicler Salimbene di Adam (1221–90):

'Foster-mothers and nurses [were commanded] to suckle and bathe and wash the children, but in no ways to prattle or speak with them; for he would have learnt whether

> *they would speak the Hebrew language (which had been*
> *the first), or Greek, or Latin, or Arabic, or perchance*
> *the tongue of their parents of whom they had been*
> *born. But he laboured in vain, for the children could not*
> *live without clappings of the hands, and gestures, and*
> *gladness of countenance, and blandishments.'*

James IV, King of Scotland between 1488 and 1513, sent two children to the remote island of Inchkeith to be raised by a mute woman. The children were reported to have begun to speak Hebrew, but the truth of this was doubted even at the time.

The Mughal Emperor Akbar the Great, who reigned in India between 1556 and 1605, believed that speech was not innate, but acquired, because children listened to others speaking. He isolated babies to discover whether children raised without speech would remain mute. It was reported that they developed a communication system based on gesture, a finding supported by more recent observations of naturally occurring isolation.

Akbar seems to have been the only person to conduct the experiment out of psychological curiosity rather than for religious or political reasons.

Frederick II reputedly attempted the 'forbidden experiment' in order to establish which language God had imparted to Adam and Eve.

TYPES OF EXPERIMENT

Experimental methods aim to examine the relationship between variable conditions. There are two main types of variable: an independent variable is a condition that is manipulated by the researcher; a dependent variable is one which changes depending on the state of the independent variables. If you want to discover the temperature at which ice cream melts, you need to examine it at different temperatures. Temperature is the independent variable, which you control. The solid/liquid state of the ice cream is the dependent variable, which changes as you change the temperature.

There are three types of experiment commonly used in psychological studies:

- *Laboratory, or controlled, experiments: the experimenter has full control over the conditions and location of the experiment. It might be carried out with human subjects, animals or biological tissue, such as nerve cells.*
- *Field experiments: the experiment takes place in the everyday world. The experimenter has control over the important independent variables, but there will be other variables outside his or her control (such as the weather), making it difficult to replicate an experiment later.*
- *Natural experiments: the experiment is really an observation of what happens in a real-world environment. The researcher has no control over variables. Natural experiments are not set up; instead the researcher notices the potential of a*

> *situation which could be studied. An example is*
> *the study of the development of children left in*
> *orphanages (see page 188).*

Feral children

Of course, the forbidden experiment is only forbidden if set up by an experimenter. There have been several 'natural experiments' involving the observation of children raised outside normal society, either because they were neglected or hidden away by abusive parents, or lost and raised by animals.

Stories of children being brought up by an animal date back thousands of years. Raised by a she-wolf, Romulus reputedly overcame his challenging start in life to achieve greatness as founder and ruler of Rome. Most feral children (including Romulus' twin brother Remus) are not so fortunate. Although many of the earlier stories cannot be verified, there have been more recent reports from the 20th and 21st centuries which describe children being brought up by dogs, wolves, monkeys, goats and even ostriches. One boy, found in India in 1979, was living an amphibious lifestyle near a river. Typically, feral children display behaviour particular to that of their 'parent' animal, including eating raw food, shunning human contact, and walking on all fours. Many of them have no human language skills (which refutes the reported results of some examples of the forbidden experiment).

'GENIE' (B.1957)
'Genie' was a young female victim of extreme abuse. Locked alone in a room from the age of 20 months to 13 years, she

was eventually discovered by child welfare officers in Los Angeles. Her father had kept her tied up, unable to move more than her toes and fingers, fed her only liquids and allowed no social contact. He had beaten her if she made a noise. When discovered, she couldn't walk, talk or eat solid food and was incontinent. After her release, she acquired rudimentary language skills and learned to walk, though with a strange stance. She was studied during attempts at rehabilitation, but in 1977 her mother, blind and unable to look after Genie herself, refused any further scientific study. Genie's father shot himself before his trial for abuse. Genie currently lives in residential care in California and is non-verbal again.

Children who have been kept secluded with animals behave in similar ways. A seven-year-old boy found in Russia in 2008 had lived all his life in a room full of birds. His only human contact was with his mother (who treated him like a bird) and he communicated by chirping and flapping his arms. This data informs the debate about how much human activity (mental and physical) is the result of heredity and how much is the result of a child's home environment (see Chapter 6).

In recent years, children who have been secluded or who have lived in the wild and subsequently been introduced into society have been closely observed during the process of their readjustment. Their terrible plight has provided rich pickings for psychologists.

UNTOLD EXPERIMENTS

As it is so easy to 'experiment' on children (or on employees or slaves), it's likely that there have been many undocumented and probably unethical tests prompted by a range of impulses – from scientific interest or the desire to live more purely to acts of callous or prurient curiosity. For example, the high-born French essayist Michel de Montaigne (1533–92) was educated to speak Latin as his first language. Another part of his father's pedagogical plan involved the child being raised for the first three years of his life in a small cottage, where he was cared for by a peasant family. The aim, according to his father, was to 'draw the boy close to the people, and to the life conditions of the people, who need our help'. Perhaps surprisingly, this upbringing created in Montaigne what he himself described as a spirit of 'liberty and delight'.

Montaigne's upbringing was based on humanist principles. Although born into a family of wealthy aristocrats, he spent his first three years living with a peasant family.

Into the breach

On the whole, however, the recorded investigation of the human mind before the 19th century was achieved through philosophical enquiry. The gap between philosophy and scientific psychology could only be bridged once some physiological knowledge was in place. This began during the 17th century, with the Scientific Revolution.

HOW GALEN GOT IT WRONG

The general idea that nerves carry information between the brain and parts of the body was not new – it is present even in the Greek philosopher Galen's accounts of physiology, written in the 2nd century AD. Neither Galen nor his successors were very clear about how the brain communicated with the body, but they seemed to think it involved some kind of moving 'spirits' travelling along the nerves, which were thought to be hollow. For 1,400 years, no one came up with a better idea.

VITALISM V. MATERIALISM

Just as philosophy struggled with the mind/body problem, physiology wrestled with the issue of whether there was anything more to the body beyond its physical structures and processes. Vitalists maintained that there was a 'life force' – something other than the physical body – but as it was not physical, it was not amenable to investigation. Materialists thought that there was nothing particularly special about life, and humans, like any other organism, can be explained in terms of physical and chemical processes.

'The Nerves are nothing else but productions of the marrowy and slimy substance of the Brain, through which the Animal spirits do rather beam than are transported. And this substance is indeed more fit for irradiation than a conspicuous or open cavity, which would have made our motions and sensations more sudden, commotive, violent and disturbed, whereas now the members receiving a gentle and successive

> *illumination are better commanded by our will and*
> *moderated by our reason.'*
>
> Helkiah Crooke (1576–1648), *Microcosmographia,*
> *a Description of the Body of Man* (1631)

Then, around 1630, René Descartes (see pages 22–4) devised a purely mechanical explanation in which the 'spirits' were replaced with fluid – a liquid, gas or 'fine flame' of some type. He still believed the nerves to be hollow, even though ten years previously the Scottish medical student John Moir had recorded in his 1620 lecture notes that: 'nerves have no perceptible cavity internally, as the veins and arteries have'.

Descartes gave the first precise explanation of how a reflex action might work. Any stimulus to a sense organ, he claimed, pulled the threads of the nerves taut. This opened a conduit in the corresponding part of the brain that allowed animal spirits to flow down the tubes to the affected area, swelling the muscles and causing them to move. Although he was wrong in all the details, the general principle is sound – a signal goes from the sensory nerves to the central nervous system, causing another signal to go to the motor nerves and move the muscles as necessary. Descartes also suggested using the word 'stimulus' for that which excites the nerves.

THE STATUES IN THE GARDEN

Descartes was inspired in his model of the nervous system by a series of automata in the gardens of St Germain, in France. These were moved by the flow of water through pipes, activated by people treading on pressure pads

> *beneath the paths. Descartes thought that if statues could be moved in that way, maybe some similar mechanism might be responsible for movement of the human body.*

Descartes' work on the body was published in 1662, twelve years after his death. It was the first advance in 1,500 years in theory relating to the nerves, but it was overturned just three years later by someone carrying out experiments rather than thinking purely theoretically.

FIRST OF THE FROGS

In the 17th century, a young Dutch physiologist, Jan Swammerdam (1637–80), carried out experiments on frogs which showed that the brain rather than the heart was involved in movement. Swammerdam then, radically, demonstrated that movement could be induced even without the brain being present. He began by removing the heart and showing the frog could still swim without it, but he found that it couldn't swim when he removed the brain. However, he demonstrated that if he stimulated a nerve with his scalpel, a leg muscle would still contract. He could even make the muscle contract if the leg had been removed from the frog. Descartes' theory that spirits travel from the brain to move the muscle mechanically was thoroughly disproven – the brain didn't even need to be in the same room for the muscle to move.

Swammerdam's experiment was one of the most important in the history of neurophysiology and psychology. The connection he made between a stimulus and a response, carried out through the action of the nerves, laid the basis for behavioural psychology: the belief that the behaviour of an organism, human or other, is entirely the result of the sum total of all the stimuli it receives.

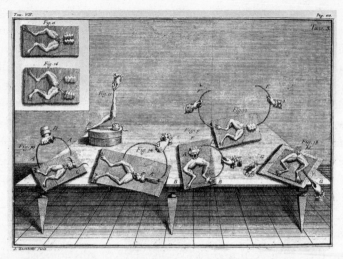

Galvani's experiment made him the first person to appreciate the relationship between electricity and animation, or life.

'From these experiments, therefore, it may, I think, be fairly concluded, that a simple and natural motion or irritation of the nerve alone is necessary to produce muscular motion, whether it has its origin in the brain, or in the marrow, or elsewhere.'

Jan Swammerdam (1678)

ANIMAL ELECTRICITY

Although Swammerdam was certain he had demonstrated that animal spirits don't exist, he had not precisely explained how the nerves carry information. He likened it to vibrations travelling through a solid, such as a plank of wood, which has been knocked. The next step was taken by the Italian scientist Luigi Galvani (1737–98). According to legend, Galvani had been skinning a dead frog at a bench where he had previously been experimenting with static electricity when an assistant touched one of the frog's nerves with a metal scalpel. The leg made a jumping movement, as though the frog was alive. Galvani went on to investigate the surprising result by passing electric currents through leg muscles and observing their movements. He concluded that 'animal electricity' was behind muscle movement in living things, and was carried by the ionization of fluids in the body. Galvani had made a startling discovery – the first in neurology.

NON-ANIMAL ELECTRICITY

Repeating Galvani's experiments, Italian physicist Alessandro Volta (1745–1827) recognized that the metal cable which Galvani had used to connect the muscles and nerves was passing the electric current between the two. Realizing that the source of the electricity was biochemical, Volta set about reproducing the effect outside the body and, as a result, developed the first battery. In this way, applying electricity to frogs started two disciplines: neurology and electrical engineering.

PUTTING TOGETHER THE PIECES

All that remained was to show how 'animal electricity' operates in the sensory and motor nerves and the brain.

This occurred in 1811 when the British physiologist Charles Bell (1774–1842) produced a pamphlet outlining his findings from anatomical experiments with rabbits. Showing unusual compassion for the times in which he lived, Bell refrained from carrying out his experiment on a live subject because he was concerned about the distress he would cause by cutting through the animal's nerves. In the end, he experimented on an unconscious rabbit.

> '*I therefore struck a rabbit behind the ear so as to deprive it of sensibility by the concussion, and then exposed the spinal marrow. On irritating the posterior roots of the nerve I could perceive no motion consequent on any part of the muscular frame; but on irritating the anterior roots of the nerve, at each touch of the forceps there was a corresponding motion of the muscles to which the nerve was distributed. These experiments satisfied me that the different roots and different columns from whence those roots arose were devoted to distinct offices, and that the notions drawn from the anatomy were correct.*'
>
> **Charles Bell (1811)**

Bell described different nerves for sensory and motor systems, connecting to the spinal cord at different places. The sensory nerves carry information from the sense organs, including sensory receptors in the skin, and enter the spinal column on the dorsal (back) side. The motor nerves connect at the ventral (front) side and carry information from the spinal column to the muscles. This confirmed that there is two-way traffic, with signals travelling to and from the brain along different routes. Unfortunately, Bell did not publicize his discovery beyond producing a pamphlet he delivered to his friends. When the French physiologist François Magendie (1783–1855) made and published the same discovery eleven years later, dispute about priority ensued.

Bell suggested that there are five types of nerve, corresponding to our five senses, but it was left to the German physiologist Johannes Müller (1801–58) to demonstrate this. In 1835, Müller found that sensory nerves are particularly suited to specific types of stimulation (the eye works best with light, for example), but he found they could also be stimulated in other ways (we can experience visual hallucinations after a knock on the head, for example). He decided that the specificity was in the nature of the nerve transmission rather than the source of the stimulus or the area of the brain that processed the signal. (In this he was wrong – Lord Edgar Adrian demonstrated in 1912 that the energy transmitted by all nerves is the same; the variation lies in where the signal comes from and how the brain processes it.) Most importantly, Müller's work demonstrated that our sense perceptions are determined internally – by the body and its nerves – not simply by the nature of the external environment.

Towards a science of the mind

By the middle of the 19th century, the basic essentials of neuroscience had been discovered. In philosophy, there had been a move towards confidence in human achievement, in science, and in the belief that the world could be made better through the application of human ingenuity and knowledge. But it was, in fact, an exercise in astronomy that prompted the first experiments in human psychology.

SLOPPY WORK OR A NEW SCIENCE?

In 1795, the Astronomer Royal, Nevil Maskelyne (1732–1811), and his assistant David Kinnebrook were making astronomical calculations by observing the point at which a star crossed a hairline in the Greenwich Observatory telescope and timing its transit. Maskelyne had chastised Kinnebrook because his timings were consistently half a second slower than Maskelyne's own. Eventually, when Kinnebrook failed to improve his performance (indeed, it grew even slower), Maskelyne dismissed him and the 24-year-old assistant returned to being a schoolteacher. It was 20 years before a German astronomer, Friedrich Bessel (1784–1846), looked again at the results and wondered if there was a personal difference in response times and that Kinnebrook had not been incompetent after all. Bessel carried out the first reaction-time study and calculated personal equations which enabled him to correct the times between observers.

Bessel's study revealed that the observer influences the outcome of observations, so this had to be taken into account with scientific observations of all types. He had also carried out the first psychology experiment into inter-personal differences. It was a field that would not gain much immediate attention, but would later become a massively important area of psychological research.

Psychophysics – getting physical with psychology

Measuring the speed of reactions was an early step in a new, quantitative approach called psychophysics – the study of physical aspects of psychology. Psychophysics looks at the physical properties of stimuli and how they relate to perception. It has many applications in modern technology – in measuring the number of colours we can distinguish, for instance, it enables development of optimum compression algorithms for images.

SPOT THE DIFFERENCE

If a sound begins below the threshold of human hearing and steadily grows in volume, there comes a point at which you begin to notice it. Before that, the sound might have some subconscious effect on you, but you are not consciously aware of it. Similarly, if you pay attention to two slightly different stimuli, there will be a point at which you can tell they are different. If they are too similar, however, you won't be able to tell them apart.

The first person to try to quantify thresholds of perception was a German physician, Ernst Heinrich Weber (1795–1878), who was working in Leipzig, Germany, in the 1830s.

One of the founders of experimental psychology, Weber explored the degree of difference that people could detect in a stimulus. He asked people to hold and compare different weights, reporting which was the heaviest. He found there had to be a difference of 3 per cent between the weights for people to be able to tell them apart – for there to be a 'just noticeable difference', or JND. Therefore, if one weight was 100 grams, a second would need to be 3 grams lighter or heavier to be detectably different. If one weighed a kilogram, the second would need to be 30 grams heavier or lighter to be perceived as different, and so on. Weber found different degrees applied to different senses, so in comparing the lengths of two lines, for example, there must be a difference of at least 1 per cent; but a comparison of musical pitches requires a difference of at least 0.6 per cent, and so on.

Weber's law states that:

$$\Delta R/R = k$$

where:

$\Delta R =$ the smallest detectable stimulus (or JND)
$R =$ the amount of existing stimulation (from the German word *Reiz*, for 'stimulus')
$k =$ a constant (which is different for each sense)

Weber also studied other aspects of thresholds of perception. Using compass points, he measured the distance between two touches on the skin that could be separately discerned, and the point at which a sensation could not be detected at all. It was a landmark in the history of psychology, for it showed that at least some aspects of the subject could be studied by quantitative scientific methods. It laid the foundations for the acceptance of experimental psychology as a field of study.

CROSSING THE THRESHOLD

Weber's work was continued by Gustav Fechner (1801–87), who had trained first as a physicist but had to resign his professorship after suffering eye damage while investigating colour and vision. He transferred his interest to the psychological process of perception. A neutral monist (see page 28), he considered bodily and conscious acts to be different aspects of a single reality and set about finding a mathematical relationship between them. He wanted to solve the mind/body problem in a way that would satisfy the materialists but also endorse his own view that consciousness was everywhere in the universe.

Fechner defined the point at which a stimulus becomes noticeable as the 'absolute threshold'. Below this point, a stimulus might still have an effect, but it would be an unconscious one. As this couldn't be measured, he started from the absolute threshold. His work resulted in the Weber–Fechner law, a refined version of Weber's conclusion:

> *'In order that the intensity of a sensation may increase in arithmetical progression, the stimulus must increase in geometrical progression.'*

This means there is a logarithmic relationship between the intensity of a stimulus and the intensity of the resulting sensation. (Logarithmic scales are used to measure very wide variations in related phenomena, such as the Richter scale for earthquakes or the decibel measure of sound.)

Where S is sensation and R is stimulus:

$$S = k \log R$$

Suppose we find that tripling the intensity of a stimulus doubles the intensity of a sensation. If we then tripled the intensity of the stimulus again, the intensity of the sensation would increase by the same amount as previously, but now it would be triple the original (even though the intensity of the stimulus is now nine times the original). Tripling the stimulus yet again makes the sensation four times the original, and so on.

Fechner felt he had achieved his aim: he had shown a measurable link between physical stimuli and a response in the psyche. Modern findings do not entirely match Fechner's 'law', however.

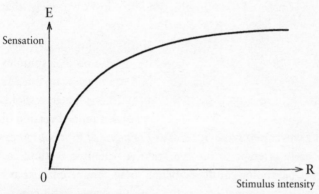

Weber–Fechner's law

GOLDEN RECTANGLES AND SPLIT CONSCIOUSNESS
Gustav Fechner conducted a study on aesthetically pleasing shapes and discovered that people found a rectangle with sides in the proportion 0.62 to be the most attractive. This corresponds to the golden ratio and the Fibonacci sequence, found everywhere in nature from the pattern in the seeds of a sunflower to the proportions of a nautilus shell. Fechner also proposed that if a brain could be split along the corpus callosum – a band of fibres that joins the two hemispheres – it would be possible to have two independent streams of

consciousness. Fechner doubted such an experiment could ever be conducted, but neuropsychologist Roger Sperry (1913–94) and psychologist Michael Gazzaniga (b.1939) did so while working in the 1960s with epileptic patients whose corpus callosum was severed to treat their condition; and they discovered that Fechner had been correct.

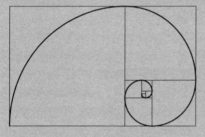

A 'golden spiral', created by drawing circular arcs in the tiles of the rectangle.

Fechner's work, published in 1860 as *Elements of Psychophysics*, was an early attempt to use quantitative scientific methods to investigate psychological phenomena. Some commentators have seen it as the beginning of psychology as a science. For others, that distinction goes to Wilhelm Wundt's founding of the first laboratory for experimental psychology (see Chapter 3).

AKA DR MISES

Fechner published several pamphlets and articles that presented his pan-psychic views and satirized aspects of the prevailing orthodoxy. As these views would have undermined his reputation as a serious scientist, he presented them under the name Dr Mises. They included titles such as The Comparative Anatomy of Angels *(1825) and* A Little Book of Life After Death *(1836).*

MEASURING THE SPEED OF THOUGHT

The German physician and physicist Hermann von Helmholtz (1821–94) was the first to make a serious attempt at measuring the speed of nerve impulses. He began with the ever-useful frogs and progressed to humans, finding that the response time depended on how far the impulse had to travel. In 1849, he carried out experiments in which he stimulated a subject's leg and asked the person to press a button when they felt the sensation. The reaction took longer when he stimulated the toe than when he stimulated the thigh. He concluded that in humans the speed of the response is 27 metres per second. In fact, the fastest human nerve transmission can be faster than a racing car, at 430 kilometres per hour (or 110 metres per second). More important than the rather variable speeds he measured was the fact that he demonstrated there *is* a speed: many people believed transmission was instantaneous, especially those who gave to God the task of realizing intention as action.

Helmholtz was also interested in Müller's findings that the sense organs can only produce their 'own' type of perception, so, for instance, a blow to the eye makes us 'see' stars. As all that the eye/brain link can do with information from the eyes is to make visual images, then that is what it does, even when it's not the most appropriate response. Helmholtz wanted to know why and how this happened and set out – ambitiously – to trace all the physiological processes involved from the moment a sensory nerve is stimulated to the point at which the sensation is recognized. It is a task that still has not been achieved.

MOVING INSIDE

Fifteen years later, the Dutch physiologist Franciscus Donders (1818–89) decided to make more complex measurements of reaction times. As well as measuring the length of time it took a subject to respond to a stimulus, he added complications. First,

Helmholtz's pendulum was used to measure the speed of a nerve impulse. The swing of the pendulum stimulates a nerve in a muscle.

he used a selection of stimuli and asked the subject to respond only to one of them, while ignoring the others. Next, he used a selection of stimuli and required a different response for each one. Subjects had to identify the stimulus and make the correct response. He found the simple stimulus/response task was the quickest, followed by the task requiring discrimination between stimuli, while the task requiring discrimination and choice was slowest. He calculated the time taken to discriminate, and the time taken to choose and respond – measurements of activity taking place entirely within the subject's brain.

With Donders' experiment, it became possible to infer activity inside the brain (or mind) from experimental data. The stage was now set for the beginnings of experimental psychology.

CHAPTER 3
How and why do we think?

'Materialist psychology... is contradicted by the fact of consciousness itself, which cannot possibly be derived from any physical qualities of material molecules or atoms.'
Wilhelm Wundt (1912)

To many people, the idea of psychology is perhaps most familiar through the image of the psychotherapist analyzing a patient, or an experiment investigating the behaviour of people or rats. From this starting point, the earliest psychology experiments would look rather alien. But they were the stepping stones to some of the most famous psychological experiments of the 20th century, some of which challenged and rewrote the way we see ourselves as humans.

Wundt and voluntarism

Wilhelm Wundt set out to understand consciousness and the mental laws which govern it. At the heart of his approach was the concept of will – the individual's choice of what to pay attention to and therefore what to perceive. He called his branch of psychology 'voluntarism', because the voluntary aspect was vital to him, though his approach would later be associated with structuralism (see page 67). Wundt experimented with human subjects, and set up the first experimental psychology laboratory in the world in order to carry out his work.

In investigating consciousness, Wundt aimed to discover the basic elements of thought, and then to establish the laws that governed their combination. His approach was through introspection, which required subjects to observe and report their own internal state. His experiments involved using various types of equipment to produce stimuli and measure reaction times, or asking subjects to reflect carefully on and report their response to a stimulus such as a light or a ticking metronome. From their reports, he tried to unpick the elements of consciousness.

Wundt's account and the input he required from his subjects look highly technical and complex. When a person experiences a stimulus there is a corresponding sensation. According to Wundt, the sensation can be broken down into modality or type – such as vision or taste – and intensity. Sensations are accompanied by emotions. These can be described in terms of three principal axes:

- pleasant/unpleasant
- excitement/calmness
- strain/relaxation

These responses are not usually experienced in isolation. It is the combination of feelings experienced together which produces perception. This is a passive process, the result of the stimulus acting on the person to produce sensations and feelings which in turn depend upon the individual's past history, personal physiology, and so on. We are not entirely governed by this passive process; within the sensations and emotions produced, we choose which elements to pay attention to, and those form our 'apperceptions'.

This is how Wundt's model works. Suppose you visit a café with two other people. For you, the strong smell of croissants brings back pleasant memories of a holiday in France. For one of your friends, the same smell will trigger different personal reflections – perhaps they were given bad news while eating fresh croissants and now the aroma has unhappy associations. For the third person, the smell has no significance – it's just a smell. You are all exposed to the same physical stimulus, your experience of sensation is the same, but the feelings that are produced are not. The perceptions and apperceptions differ from one person to another. You might delight in the smell and rejoice in the pleasant memories, the second person might try to blot out the experiences the smell recalls, and the third person does not have the smell as part of their current apperception at all.

WILHELM WUNDT (1832–1920)
Wundt was born into a family of middle-class intellectuals in Mannheim, Germany. His one surviving brother was sent away to school, so Wundt grew up without companions of his own age. Although not a promising student at school, he went on to excel in his study of medicine, graduating as a doctor from the University of Heidelberg in 1856. He joined

the university staff and worked as an assistant to Hermann Helmholtz, teaching a laboratory course in physiology. However, his main interest was psychology, and he began writing Principles of Physiological Psychology, *now regarded as the first textbook on experimental psychology, in 1874.*

He transferred to the University of Leipzig, where, after some struggle, he set up the first laboratory specifically devoted to psychological studies, which immediately attracted students from all over the world who were eager to learn the new science. His laboratory grew and was eventually given its own building in 1897. Wundt's structured analysis of the human mind separated psychology from philosophy by way of objective measurement and control. On the basis of his work and his influence on practitioners who followed him, he is regarded as the father of experimental psychology.

REACHING THE LIMIT

Wundt believed that introspection could unravel the basic thought elements, helping us to understand consciousness and what is going on in the mind at any particular moment. But he held that higher mental processes were beyond this type of analysis. He also believed that psychological processes, like physical processes, are subject to specific laws so complex and dependant on so many unmeasurable and unobservable factors, that prediction is impossible.

Although Wundt said we can't predict what will happen in the mind, we can sometimes unpick what has happened after the event and explain it; we can even recognize its inevitability. This looking-backwards approach would later become fundamental to psychoanalysis.

Later critics objected that while Wundt applied scientific rigour to the methods of experimentation, introspection could never be a valid scientific tool because it is not possible to measure or observe it objectively. The later behaviourists avoided this problem by working with measurable behaviours and refusing to examine the mental acts which produce them. Even so, Wundt's interest in thoughts and consciousness prepared the ground for the cognitive psychology that emerged in the second half of the 20th century.

Structuralism

Many of the large number of students who flocked to Wundt's laboratory went on to found psychology departments in other universities. One of these was Edward Titchener (1867–1927), a newly-graduated doctoral student of Wundt's, who became a professor at Cornell University in New York.

While Wundt wanted to explain the mind and its mental processes, Titchener only wanted to describe them with scientific precision. He felt that explanation was beyond the realm of science, and his brand of experimental psychology was thoroughly scientific. He called his approach 'structuralism', as he sought to investigate the structure of the mind. His interests lay only in consciousness, with no regard to the unconscious mind or instincts.

Titchener developed Wundt's ideas of introspection and mental elements, but his versions were considerably changed. Instead of just noting whether they did or did not respond to a stimulus, Titchener's subjects were asked to observe their response and describe it in elemental terms, breaking it down as far as possible. For example, rather than naming an object presented to them, subjects were asked to report their sensations – describing the object as warm, heavy, red, and so on.

Titchener determined that the elements of consciousness are 'sensations' (elements of perceptions), 'images' (elements of ideas) and 'affections' (elements of emotions). He distinguished more than 40,000 sensations, most of them relating to sight. Studying sensations took up most of his time. He measured them in terms of quality, duration, intensity, clarity and 'extensivity' (to what degree a sensation extends over an area or space). He applied the same attributes to ideas. For emotions, as far as he was concerned, the only meaningful attribute was pleasantness/unpleasantness. He believed all previous experiences come into play when we give sense to something. This is based on association – the action of the mind making associations between experiences which occur close together, or which are frequently encountered together. Titchener rejected Wundt's theory of apperception.

For all its detailed structure and focus on scientific rigour (in part, because of them) Titchener's approach did not survive his death. It left out too much that was becoming important in psychology, and its reliance on introspection was itself problematic. Some critics pointed out that it was really retrospection, as the mental event had happened by the time the subject described it. The account of introspection was impure: it was tainted or distorted by memory, and even by the act of looking at it. The type of objective scientific method that Titchener wanted to use to explore psychology didn't really seem to work, at least not when applied in this way.

Functionalism

While Titchener was developing his structuralist approach to the mind, one of the most influential American psychologists, William James (1842–1910), was developing a different method. 'Functionalism' focused not on the static structure of the mind, but on the function or purpose of mental processes. It related the activity of the mind to Darwinian evolution and took a more holistic, integrated approach: how did the mind work to help the individual survive?

FUNCTIONALISM AND EVOLUTION

The functionalist school of psychology developed from the theory of evolution. The central tenet of functionalism was that the actions of the mind have a function, and this function has served to make the organism better-suited to its environment and the life it must live.

WILLIAM JAMES (1842–1910)

Born into a wealthy and influential New York family, William James was exposed to the ideas of many great thinkers of the day. His education took place partly in the USA and partly in Europe, and he became fluent in French and German. At first, he wanted to be an artist, but his father so disapproved that James changed his mind and decided to train in science, enrolling at Harvard in 1861. In 1864 he transferred to Harvard Medical School. Although he qualified as a doctor, he never practised medicine.

In early adult life, James suffered several forms of physical illness (after eight months, he had to abandon an Amazonian expedition with the Swiss naturalist Louis Agassiz because of seasickness and mild smallpox) as well as psychological symptoms, including depression. His depression was eventually alleviated when he discovered a philosophical position which provided meaning for him.

James remained at Harvard for the rest of his life, establishing psychology as a field of study there and setting up the first teaching laboratory in the subject anywhere in the world. His students included US President Theodore Roosevelt, the Spanish philosopher George Santayana and the American novelist Gertrude Stein.

After publishing his seminal work, Principles in Psychology *(1890), James wanted to move away from experimental psychology to concentrate more on philosophy and psychic phenomena. He helped found the American Society for Psychical Research in 1884.*

As the name suggests, functionalism was concerned with the functioning of the mind – its action and what its action is used for. Instead of looking only at the mainstream – the psychology of normal, adult humans – functionalism also examined animal behaviour, child psychology and abnormal psychology. As the environment for each person is different, the characteristics that make one person suited to their environment are not necessarily the same as the characteristics that make another person suited to theirs – such as patience in a driving instructor or competitiveness in a stock broker. Consequently, functionalism was equally concerned with differences between people and with the common ground they share.

PUTTING IT TO USE

Because it is preoccupied with how and why the mind works as it does, functionalism has a clear interest in the uses of mental processes and behaviours. The functionalists were interested in psychology as a practical science with useful applications, rather than as a pure science (knowledge for its own sake). In functionalism, we find the origins of the applications that attempt to use psychology to make people's lives better: improving education, work and the treatment of the sick, for example. Intelligence testing became an important strand in applied psychology during the early 20th century. Functionalism, then, was broadly pragmatic – a point of clear distinction from the structuralists, who avoided any practical application of psychological knowledge.

THE BIRTH OF AMERICAN PSYCHOLOGY

The publication of *Principles of Psychology* by William James marked the point at which American psychology broke away from philosophy and from European traditions in psychology. Running to nearly 1,400 pages, the *Principles* set out a view in opposition to Wundt's. The brother of the novelist Henry James, William taught at Harvard where he set up a teaching laboratory in 1875. Although established four years later, Wundt's laboratory is generally considered the first because it was experimental, whereas James' was used exclusively for demonstrations.

James popularized the phrase 'stream of consciousness'. He believed that consciousness was continuous, from birth to death, and constantly changing. It could therefore not be divided or stopped for psychologists to take a look at it. The 'elements of consciousness' approach taken by Wundt was meaningless in James' view. Furthermore, the importance of consciousness for the individual is that it aids survival. Its decision about which things to attend to (or not) is governed by what things are useful to the individual.

James was convinced that instincts and habits are behaviours useful to the organism, whether animal or human. Habits, he believed, are behaviours that have been reinforced during the course of the individual's life. By repetition, they become entrenched and are then less costly in terms of conscious effort.

> 'Consciousness, then, does not appear to itself chopped up in bits. Such words as "chain" or "train" do not describe it fitly as it presents itself in the first instance. It is nothing jointed; it flows. A "river" or "stream" are the metaphors by which it is most naturally described. In talking of it hereafter, let us call it the stream of thought, of consciousness, or of subjective life.'
>
> William James (1890)

FREE WILL

James initially struggled with the concept of free will. As a young man, he was thrown into despair by the determinism he saw as an inevitable consequence of accepting the theory of evolution. If the materialist view of psychology that he had learned in Germany was correct, then everything a human did was an inevitable consequence of a neurophysiological state which had developed over the course of evolution. There was, then, no freedom in human action, and no hope or choice in life.

James then read an essay by the French philosopher Charles Renouvier (1815–1903), which persuaded him that he might freely choose to attend to one thought rather than another when several were available to him. This had a significant impact on James' psychological theories. He decided that in choosing which thoughts to attend to, we determine both our personalities and the actions we take. The actions we take determine how we feel – which is counterintuitive, as we usually suppose that our actions stem from how we feel rather than the other way around.

Suppose you see a bear approaching you in the woods and you run away. You might think you are running away because you are frightened – but, according to James, you are frightened because you have run away. The body acts instinctively to run away from the dangerous bear and the brain interprets the running away as signalling fear, so you feel frightened. The suggestion that you act in order to control how you feel stems from the belief that our emotions take their cues from our behaviour. Consequently, if you are miserable, smiling in spite of your misery will eventually cheer you up. Experiments exploring cognitive dissonance (see Chapter 6), carried out in the 20th century by social psychologists Leon Festinger and James Merrill Carlsmith, seem to support James' view.

THE RISE OF PRAGMATISM

In his later years, James became increasingly interested in parapsychology and sought a replacement for his work at Harvard so that he could focus on this work. He was succeeded by Hugo Münsterberg (1863–1916), a German-born psychologist who was deeply unimpressed by James' forays into mysticism, parapsychology and the newly emerging psychoanalysis. He felt that these subjects had no place in psychology, which he considered an eminently practical science. Indeed, he completely dismissed the unconscious that was central to psychoanalysis and to James' parapsychology interests. Münsterberg's work focused on aspects of psychology which he believed would be of practical use in the world, initiating the fields of forensic psychology (that applies psychology to criminality) and industrial psychology (that applies psychology to the workplace).

Münsterberg was the first to consider how psychology could be applied to legal cases, arguing that brutal interrogation of criminals would not yield useful results because it would lead suspects to give unreliable accounts. For example, they might say what they thought the interrogator wanted to hear, rather than the truth, in order to end the questioning, or they might be innocent and yet lie in order to seek punishment because of underlying depressive issues. Münsterberg outlined a design for a device that would expose the telling of untruths by measuring physiological changes in the subject, such as an altered pulse or rate of breathing. His train of thought would eventually lead to the development of the lie detector.

> *'The story of the subconscious mind can be told in three words: there is none.'*
>
> Hugo Münsterberg (1909)

In the USA in the early 1950s, a murder suspect takes a lie detector test.

Functionalism comes of age

The American philosopher and psychologist John Dewey (1859–1952) took functionalism and pragmatism in new directions and called his version of psychology 'instrumentalism'. Initially a teacher and then a philosopher, Dewey brought to psychology a strong interest in pedagogy. Following James' lead, he believed that dividing consciousness into stages was invalid, but went beyond James in saying that dividing behaviour into elements was invalid. Dewey believed the functionalist school ignored the continuity of human behaviour and its significance in terms of adaptation. He argued that the accepted way of dividing a reflex action into three parts – sensory process, brain process, motor process – was not useful, since it didn't take account of the integrated nature of an experience. Using the example of a child touching a flame, feeling pain, and withdrawing from the flame, he pointed out that the most important part of the sequence is that the child learns that flames can hurt and his or her future behaviour is modified by this knowledge.

Dewey saw the adaptive function of experience as vital, and considered that all behaviour should be viewed in this way – in terms of its function in helping the individual adapt to their environment. The adaptation was to make the organism more fit to survive.

A liberal, who believed that all philosophy and psychology must have practical applications, Dewey supported women's suffrage, democracy, the rights of black people, intellectual freedom and progressive education. He also directed the Dewey Commission which was held in Mexico in 1937; this found Leon Trotsky innocent of the crimes of which he had been accused by Joseph Stalin.

In 1906, James Rowland Angell (1869–1949) took over from Dewey as president of the American Psychological Association. He argued that the functional psychologist was interested in 'mental activity as part of a larger stream of biological forces'. In this manner, functional psychologists aligned themselves with evolutionary biology; they saw mental processes aiding in adaptation and helping the organism to survive.

Angell argued that mind and body are an inseparable unit, working together for the survival of the organism. By making the strong link with evolutionary theory, he led functionalists to embrace animal behaviour and child psychology as useful tools adding experimental techniques.

THE ADAPTIVE ACT

The American psychologist Harvey Carr (1873–1954) explained the 'adaptive act' at the heart of the functionalist approach. It comprises three components:

- a stimulus (such as thirst, or the need to escape danger)
- a specific environmental setting
- a response which satisfies the motivating need

The environment is important because it affects the need – seeing a bear in a zoo is not the same as seeing a bear when you are walking in the woods. The organism learns that the response has satisfied the need, and will resort to it again when the same need arises – the act is adaptive, helping the organism to survive with minimal effort. This is the last meaningful part of the child-burned-by-fire jigsaw.

Psychoanalysis and the psychodynamic approach

At much the same time as functionalism emerged in the United States, a new movement in Europe rejected the objective approach altogether. In a consulting room in Vienna, Sigmund Freud was developing the process of psychoanalysis, putting together his theories about the unconscious mind and how early experiences determine character. Freud's approach began as a therapeutic endeavour to help patients suffering mental distress, but it soon developed into a theory about the structure and workings of the mind. His methods were entirely subjective, involving in-depth conversations, or analysis, with individuals. His theories are based primarily on case studies. This approach has clear shortcomings, as Freud based his ideas about the mind in general on a small sample of similar people (middle-class, 19th-century citizens of Vienna) and exclusively on people who already appeared to be suffering from mental distress.

Psychoanalysis was not the only psychodynamic method to appear at this time. The Austrian medical doctor Alfred Adler (1870–1937) developed a method he called 'Individual Psychology'. Like Freud, he believed that actions and mental states are determined by earlier experiences. But while Freud saw sexuality and the sex drive as central, Adler saw the 'inferiority complex' as the most important element in determining adult character, problems and behaviour.

It is important to note that all psychodynamic approaches are highly deterministic: they make events and influences early in life responsible for what happens to a person later, robbing the individual of agency.

The indivisible whole

Throughout the 1890s and early 1900s, psychology was dominated by polar opposite approaches – the functionalist and psychodynamic schools – on either side of the Atlantic. Then, at almost the same time, two new movements emerged. Both took the problems with structuralism and functionalism as their starting points. One was Gestalt psychology, from the German word *gestalt*, meaning 'shape' or 'whole'; the other was behaviourism.

Gestalt psychology rejected the idea of breaking consciousness or stimuli and responses into constituent elements and the inevitable fragmentation of experience that resulted from this. The Gestaltists claimed that it did not reflect how we experience the world; the conscious experience is felt, they said, and must be studied as a unified whole. We don't see the parts of a dog and piece them together to understand that there is a dog present – we recognize what we see and hear as a dog all in one go. The Gestaltists concentrated on phenomena – entire, experienced, internal or external events and behaviours. They demonstrated this using experimental methods.

SEEING THE LIGHT

The origins of Gestalt psychology are generally credited to the Austro–Hungarian psychologist Max Wertheimer (1880–1943), who developed the theory on a train journey between Vienna and the Rhineland in 1910. When an idea about the nature of perception occurred to him, he got off the train at Frankfurt and bought a toy stroboscope, which flashed a sequence of pictures in rapid succession to give the impression of a moving image. In his Frankfurt hotel room, he experimented with how the speed of perceiving a sequence of images can produce the perception of movement, although this is not the movement (that of the stroboscope) which is actually taking place.

Later, in his laboratory, Wertheimer experimented with equipment which could flash lights on and off at differing speeds. He found that by varying the speed of two alternately flashing lights he could produce the perception that one light was permanently on, or was flashing on and off, or was moving between two points (this last is called the 'phi phenomenon'). The eyes, therefore, can lie: what we 'perceive' is not necessarily what we 'see'.

Gestalt psychology begins with the perceived event or experience and works to determine what produced it and how.

This contrasts with other methods which gather what are believed to be the components of perception or experience and then build with them.

Wertheimer worked closely with the German psychologists Kurt Koffka (1886–1941) and Wolfgang Köhler (1887–1967), who were originally his test subjects for phi phenomenon studies of apparent movement, which led the three men to conclusions about the inherent nature of vision. Wertheimer, Koffka and Köhler are often cited as the joint originators of Gestalt psychology.

THE CIRCLE AND THE MELODY

The Austrian philosopher Christian von Ehrenfels (1859–1932) discussed the relationship between the elements of sensory perception and our understanding of the whole experience. For example, he described the way in which we experience a melody in its entirety rather than attending to the individual notes. If the melody is transposed into a different key we still perceive it as the same melody, even though the individual notes are different. (The same notes could also be reused in a different melody, of course.) This he called the *Gestalt-qualität*, the 'qualities of a whole', and which we add somehow in the act of perception.

A pupil of Ehrenfels, Wertheimer was inspired by him. He developed the theory further, saying, 'What is given me by the melody does not arise . . . as a secondary process from the sum of the pieces as such. Instead, what takes place in each single part already depends upon what the whole is.' So, we first hear the melody and only afterwards might divide it up into notes. Wertheimer found an example in vision, too. If we look at a circle, we see it first in its entirety, as a circle, and only afterwards notice how it is made up. We see the circle 'im-mediately' – that is, not mediated by a process of adding together the parts.

GESTALT SPY: HAS MONKEYS, WILL TRAVEL

In 1913, the German psychologist Wolfgang Köhler went to Tenerife in the Canary Islands to study chimpanzees. He worked there for six years. There has been speculation, reinforced by reports by two of his children and the man who looked after his experimental animals, that during World War I Köhler spied for the Germans. With a concealed radio, he is said to have notified the German Navy of any Royal Navy activity in the area. Once the coast was clear, German ships could enter the area to refuel.

Köhler's research into chimpanzee behaviour concluded that the animals exhibit insight and intelligent behaviour also common in humans. It marked a turning point in the psychology of thinking. He wrote a book on problem-solving entitled The Mentality of Apes *(1917), describing his belief that people should not underestimate the influence of external conditions on higher animals such as apes.*

Köhler wrote several articles publicly attacking the Nazi regime, but somehow evaded arrest. However, in 1935, after speaking out against the persecution of the Jews and refusing to begin his lectures by giving the Nazi salute, he left Germany for good to live and work in the USA.

HOW IT WORKS

Wertheimer and the other Gestaltists proposed a mechanism by which sensory impressions are transformed by the mind into whole perceptions. The mind, they claimed, has pre-existing electrochemical fields which act on incoming sense perceptions in a way that is comparable with a magnetic field acting on iron particles. Mental activity results from the interaction of sensory data with force-fields in the brain; this mental activity forms configurations that are experienced as perception.

THE GESTALT PRINCIPLES

According to Gestalt psychology, the brain will always tend towards an interpretation that is as simple, symmetrical and well-organized as circumstances allow. This can be demonstrated experimentally by showing people various images and asking what they see. The Gestaltists found that when we look at a figure, we try to recognize in it some kind of order. So, if we look at the following diagram –

Fig.1

we organize it into an overlapping triangle and square; we don't see a jumble of lines and angles. The Gestaltists called this the law of *prägnanz* ('precision'). It has given rise to several laws of Gestalt which explain how we organize visual perception to create order from apparent chaos.

The law of proximity leads us to see objects that are close to one another as groups. It means we see the circles in the diagram on the right as three groups of 12 rather than 36 discrete circles.

Fig.2

The law of similarity leads us to group things together if they are alike. In the diagram on the right, we see three rows of white circles and three rows of black circles, rather than just a block of 36 circles.

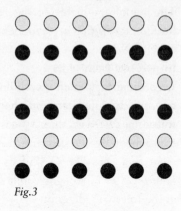

Fig.3

The law of symmetry or 'good form' makes us group together objects that are of similar pattern, colour, shape, and so on. It means that we see the next figure as three sets of symmetrical brackets, not six separate brackets:

Fig.4

The law of closure leads us to see completed, anticipated shapes. So we will consider the figure on the right to be a circle with a broken outline, rather than a series of curved lines.

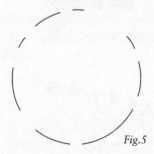

Fig.5

Fig.6

Closure or reification is the tendency to see a recognizable object even when it is not there. In the figure on the left, we see a complete shape, a white triangle, rather than three black circles with sections cut out.

The law of good continuation says that we perceive shapes and lines together if they form an object that is simple, regular and concise. Where there is an intersection between objects, we tend to perceive each object as single and uninterrupted. Therefore, we see Fig.1 as a square and a triangle overlapping or joined, not an irregular shape with eight sides. We also see the following images as two lines that cross rather than four lines that meet:

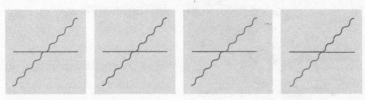

Fig.7

The law of common fate makes us group objects if they move together at the same rate and in the same direction. The groups of birds, below, are identical; but we perceive them as two discrete objects because the continuity of movement in the top group is opposite to that of the bottom group.

Fig.8

The law of past experience can overrule the other laws. It draws on what we already know to help us interpret what we see. If we are reading text and come across 'OO', we are likely to interpret this as letters – double 'O'. But if we are looking at a page of figures, we are more likely to see 'OO' as a number – double zero or '00'.

Fig.9

EMERGENCE, MULTISTABILITY AND INVARIANCE

The Gestalt principle of emergence is the tendency to see a recognizable image in an abstract pattern of lines or shapes. For example, you may be able to see a Dalmatian dog in the picture on the left. Once you've recognized the dog, it is hard to 'unsee' it.

Multistability stems from a confusion between the background and foreground of an image. When it seems that part of a picture could be either foreground or background, our minds switch frantically between the two, as in the famous Rubin face on the right. Is it a vase or two human faces in profile?

Fig.10

Invariance is our ability to recognize an object as being the same even after it has been rotated, inverted or otherwise seemingly altered, or if it is seen at a distance or cast in shadow (see Fig.11). Indeed, we are so ready to identify familiar and particularly human forms that there is even a name –pareidolia – for the tendency that leads us to 'see' a human face in the rocks on Mars or the craters of the Moon.

Gestalt psychology is not concerned with explaining how these features of perception come

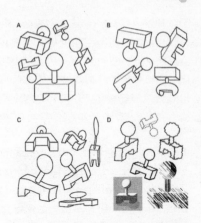

Fig.11

about but only in recognizing that they do and that this governs how we perceive the world. The rise of Nazism in Germany meant that, by 1935, all the major protagonists of Gestalt psychology had left Europe to live in the USA.

No dividing line between man and brute

On the other side of the Atlantic, in 1913, the year after Wertheimer embarked on the path to Gestalt, John B. Watson (1878–1958) outlined the main features of his new philosophy of psychology called 'behaviourism' in an influential article, 'Psychology as the Behaviorist Views It'. His emphasis on people's external behaviours and their reactions to given situations, rather than their internal mental state, initially met with criticism but Watson persisted. The article, sometimes called 'The Behaviorist Manifesto' set out his stall:

> *'Psychology as the behaviorist views it is a purely objective experimental branch of natural science. Its theoretical goal is the prediction and control of behavior. Introspection forms no essential part of its methods, nor is the scientific value of its data dependent upon the readiness with*

which they lend themselves to interpretation in terms of consciousness. The behaviorist, in his efforts to get a unitary scheme of animal response, recognizes no dividing line between man and brute. The behavior of man, with all of its refinement and complexity, forms only a part of the behaviorist's total scheme of investigation.'

Behaviourism was not interested in the inaccessible internal events of the mind. Indeed, many committed behaviourists denied the validity of the concept of 'mind', and said the mind didn't exist. Watson was inclined, initially at least, to an epiphenomenalist view (this position holds that mental states are by-products of events in the brain, but have no effect upon the brain or the body to which the brain is connected). Later, Watson would also take a monist view, insisting that everything was physical. He stated:

'[Consciousness] has never been seen, touched, smelled, tasted, or moved. It is a plain assumption, just as unprovable as the old concept of the soul.'

Instead, the behaviourist would approach human experience and nature purely through what could be observed and measured – behaviour.

Behaviourism wasn't immediately popular. It represented a significant shift in traditional forms of psychology, so took a while to catch on. But when it did, it came to dominate the field for a large part of the 20th century, going more or less unchallenged as the most important school for around 40 years. Some of the most famous and ground-breaking experiments in 20th-century psychology were behaviourist projects.

Watson began with an interest in Pavlov's findings in classical conditioning, using dogs as experimental animals (see panel below). Watson took instincts, reflexes and conditioning as his starting point and set out to explain all human behaviour in that model. Accordingly, he spent a lot of time working with young children, in whom it is easiest to see instincts clearly at work because they are unclouded by the fog of extensive experience and learning. He and other behaviourists – such as Edward Thorndike, Edward Tolman and B. F. Skinner – valued work with animals, too.

DROOLING TO ORDER

Classical conditioning was famously discovered by the Russian physiologist Ivan Pavlov (1849–1936), who developed his 'conditioned reflex' concept around 1901. Initially investigating the reflex that leads dogs to salivate and produce stomach juices in response to the smell or taste of meat, Pavlov moved on to train the dogs to expect food when they were exposed to a certain stimulus, such as the sound of a bell, metronome or whistle. Once the dogs associated the sound with the food, they would salivate on hearing it, even if the food was not present. This idea of conditioning as an automatic form of learning influenced the behaviourist psychologists who succeeded Pavlov (as well as Aldous Huxley, who drew on it for his dystopian novel, Brave New World*).*

JOHN BROADUS WATSON (1878–1958)

Born in South Carolina to a fiercely religious mother and an alcoholic father, John B. Watson was given his unusual middle name in honour of a Baptist minister. He was raised according to harsh religious rules. His experience of this, and of his mother's passionate condemnation of smoking, drinking and dancing, left him with an abiding hatred for religion and he would become a lifelong atheist. When Watson was 13 years old, his father left the family and went to live with two Cherokee women.

Described as lazy and insubordinate, Watson was not a good student. He was twice arrested during his school years (once for fighting with African Americans, and once for discharging a gun in a public place). Nevertheless, through his mother's contacts he managed to secure a place at Furman University in Greenville, South Carolina, and graduated successfully.

After a year spent working as a school janitor, he went to the University of Chicago to study philosophy under John Dewey (see page 75). He gained his PhD for a study of the learning process in white rats, and married while he was at graduate school. In 1909, he became editor of the Psychological Review, *succeeding the eminent psychologist James Mark Baldwin, who had been fired after being caught in a raid on a brothel. Watson used the position to publish his views on behaviourism, but lost his own position at Johns Hopkins University in 1920 after having an affair with his graduate student/research assistant Rosalie Rayner.*

Watson and his wife divorced and he married Rayner in 1920, but their happiness was relatively short-lived as she died in 1935, aged just 36.

After being forced to leave academia, Watson carved out a career in advertising. He began at the bottom, in a job offered by a contact of E. B. Titchener, but went on to be phenomenally successful. At the advertising agency J. Walter Thompson, he brought his extensive knowledge of human behaviour and psychology to bear on the business of selling – the first time that psychology had been applied in advertising. Within two years, he was vice president. He continued to publish, though now in the popular press and in books for the general reader, largely on childcare. He is particularly famous for the 'Little Albert' experiment (see pages 141–2) and for his approach to parenting, which he felt should be a business-like arrangement not sullied by affection between parent and child.

COMPARATIVE PSYCHOLOGY

The behaviourists were the first psychologists to make extensive studies using animals. With methods which depended on introspection, such as those of the structuralist and functionalist schools, animals were obviously unsuitable subjects. For the behaviourists, however, they were ideal. There was no possibility of the subjects modifying their behaviour to please or frustrate a researcher, no way the researcher could influence behaviour unfairly, and no temptation to look for mental events behind the manifest behaviour. Many of the behaviourists, Watson included, worked with white rats (a favourite laboratory animal because they are clever, small, easy to look after and reach maturity quite quickly). Edward Tolman worked with rats (see page 94); Edward Thorndike (see pages 143–4) worked with cats; and B. F. Skinner worked with rats and pigeons (see pages 144–8).

'Let it be noted that rats live in cages; they do not go on binges the night before one has planned an experiment; they do not kill each other off in wars . . . they do not go

> *in for either class conflicts or race conflicts; they avoid politics, economics and papers on psychology. They are marvellous, pure and delightful.'*
>
> Edward Tolman (1945)

ACTING WITH A PURPOSE

In 1920, William McDougall (1871–1938), a British-born psychologist, took up the chair of psychology at Harvard University and focused his attention on purposive behaviour-ism. He believed that behaviour initiated by an individual, which was not a response to an identifiable stimulus, was hard to account for without considering the possibility of the involvement of something resembling the mind. McDougall distinguished purposive behaviour as:

- goal oriented;
- not initiated by an environmental stimulus;
- variable – experimenting with different ways of reaching a goal;
- persistent – not ceasing until the goal is reached or the behaviour is stopped by an environmental stimulus;
- improving – getting better at achieving the goal, through trial and error or with practice.

In place of the external stimuli which prompt reflexive behaviour, McDougall cited instinctual motives as the drive behind purposive behaviour. In its simplest form, this could be the instinct to find food when hungry. An instinct produces a number of changes: in perception (noticing food when hungry); in behaviour (doing things to get or find food); and in emotion (feeling positive towards events related to getting food, such as the suggestion of visiting a restaurant). Most of the time, however, instincts do not act alone but in configurations. Two or more instincts associated with an idea form a sentiment. McDougall's list of instincts included escape, repulsion, mating, curiosity, food-seeking, assertion, laughter, parental protection and combat.

Watson rejected instincts as part of human psychology and argued that all learning could be accounted for by associations. This theory was based on his interpretation of classical (Pavlovian) conditioning and put him at odds with McDougall, who thought learning was based on reinforcement – the repetition of behaviours found to be successful in meeting goals. In 1929, the two men had a famous debate in Washington DC, each putting his case forcefully. McDougall, who had pointed out that Watson's model couldn't account for the pleasure of listening to violin music, won by a narrow margin. However, some of his views, including those propounded in his 1920 foray into evolutionary theory entitled *The Group Mind*, together with his interest in eugenics, have led many mainstream psychologists to accuse him of scientific racism.

'I come into this hall and see a man on this platform scraping the guts of a cat with hairs from the tail of a horse; and, sitting silently in attitudes of rapt attention, are a thousand persons who presently break out into wild applause. How will the Behaviorists explain these strange incidents? . . . Common sense and psychology agree in accepting the explanation that the audience heard the music with keen pleasure. . . . But the Behaviorist knows nothing of pleasure and pain, or admiration and gratitude. He has relegated all such "metaphysical entities" to the

> *dust heap, and must seek some other explanation. Let us*
> *leave him seeking it. The search will keep him harmlessly*
> *occupied for some centuries to come.'*
>
> **William McDougall (1929)**

MORE BEHAVIOURISM

Watson was a positivist: he believed objective data to be the only valid and reliable goal of science. He wanted psychology to be put to use in predicting patterns of behaviour and suggesting ways of controlling them (his career in advertising demonstrated this interest in action). But the two aims were not entirely compatible because if he couldn't explain the behaviours he observed, how was he to use them to make predictions? The only (very limited) possibility for Watson was classical conditioning.

Another answer, for behaviourism in general, came from logical positivism. Under behaviourists such as Edward Tolman (1886–1959), Clark Leonard Hull (1884–1952) and B. F. Skinner (1904–90), behaviourism moved away from the atomistic, discrete, micro-behaviours of Watson's studies and began to encompass whole behaviours such as (in Tolman's words): 'a man driving home to dinner or a child hiding from a stranger.'

COGNITION MAKES A COMEBACK

Ultimately Tolman accepted purpose and cognition as part of his behaviourist model by describing three 'variables'. An event in the environment (independent variable) would cause some internal mental event (intervening variable) which would then result in an observable behaviour (dependent variable). Through his tests on rats, Tolman established that they could learn facts about the world that they could subsequently use in a flexible way, rather than depending on an automatic response to stimuli.

Therefore, internal events could be defined logically as they were tied to observable behaviour.

By involving purpose and cognition in his model, Tolman was moving away from the behaviourist model championed by Watson and towards the cognitive school that developed later in the 20th century. Unfortunately, his theory introduced such a degree of complexity, with its numerous intervening variables, that it was not possible for him to process all the information in an era before powerful computers. Tolman's influence endures in the popularity of cognitive behaviour therapy (CBT), which has developed at least in part from his model of purposive behaviour and mental constructs.

LOGICAL POSITIVISM

Positivism teaches that we must rely on empirical evidence. It was at the heart of science for many centuries, but by the early 20th century it was no longer possible to account for everything by referring only to directly observable phenomena. Developments in science that required, for example, an account of the structure of the atom or of magnetism, could not progress without employing some ideas which could not (then or now) be shown directly. A group of philosophers meeting in Vienna in the mid-1920s came up with a solution. Named 'logical positivism' by the Austrian philosopher Herbert Feigl (1902–88), it allowed theoretical terms as long as they could be tied to empirical evidence using rigorous logic.

LATENT LEARNING

Tolman's behavioural studies with rats led him to conclude that we are learning all the time, but putting that learning into action is latent until needed. Tolman's rats learned to negotiate a maze, whether they needed to or not. If they were put in the maze when sated with food, they would notice where the food was located but wouldn't go to it or eat it. If they were returned to the maze later on when hungry, they would go straight to the food because they had already learned where it was.

Tolman proposed that the rats built up a cognitive map of the world around them developed through a pattern of hypothesis-building and mental trial and error. When a hypothesis was confirmed it became more firmly embedded, eventually becoming a belief. He emphasized the learning of links between stimuli, so rather than an S-R (stimulus-response) theory, his can be seen as a S1-S2 (stimulus-stimulus) theory.

DRIVE REDUCTION

Another development in behaviourism came from Clark Leonard Hull, who believed that reinforcement was key to learning. In his model, a biological need creates a drive and any behaviour that diminishes the drive is reinforced. For example, if you feel hot and want (biological drive) to become cooler, you begin the cooling process by taking your jumper off, which reduces the drive. In this way, you learn to take off your jumper when you get too hot, and repeated reinforcement leads to habit. With its intervening variable between stimulus and behaviour, Hull's model resembles Tolman's, but differs in a crucial sense because the intervening variable is physiological (a biological drive) rather than mental.

RADICAL BEHAVIOURISM

B. F. Skinner was the most famous of the behaviourists and one of the most important psychologists of the 20th century. Like Watson, he took the position that mental events, even as some kind of intervening variable, were an irrelevance. He believed free will to be an illusion and thought human action depended on the consequences of previous actions. If there were any mental events, he argued, they weren't accessible to the psychologist so nothing would be gained by studying them. He saw no place in science for the 'self' and whatever mental events it might experience.

Like many of his contemporaries, Skinner experimented with rats, using them to study learning in response to stimuli. Skinner called his approach 'radical behaviourism'. He used a specially designed box which allowed him to try a variety of stimuli to determine how the rats learned best. Skinner felt that behaviourism should have practical uses and benefits for society, and gave educational advice based on the evidence of his experiments. Furthermore, he promoted the use of behaviour modification as a form of therapy for people with unwanted behaviours such as addiction, phobias and social disorders. He believed the reason that people displayed these behavioural traits was because they had gained some form of reinforcement for them in the past. It was therefore necessary to reinforce alternative types of behaviour in order to remedy the unwanted ones.

> 'A completely independent science of subjective experience would have no more bearing on a science of behaviour than a science of what people feel about fire would have on the science of combustion.'
>
> B. F. Skinner (1974)

Putting the human first

The behaviourists had conducted a great deal of their work through experiments using animal subjects. It was a central tenet of behaviourism that animal learning and human learning were comparable, because it was all down to biology. Because most behaviourists were not concerned with mental events, and generally denied the existence of them, it was often easier and just as valid to experiment with animals as it was with people. That would not hold for the two schools of psychology that emerged in the second half of the 20th century. Both were exclusively concerned with aspects of human cognition and mental structures.

The first school, that of humanistic psychology, set out to explore such topics as how we see and mould ourselves as human beings, how we find meaning in life, what drives us, and what it means to be human. It is concerned with motivation, personal growth, goals and the self. Clearly, cats, rats and pigeons in puzzle boxes are not going to help with this endeavour.

The humanistic approach to psychology originates with the work of Abraham Maslow (1908–70). Born in Brooklyn, New York, to a poor family and a mother he grew to hate, he was the oldest of seven children. As a child he was classified as mentally unstable, and suffered anti-Semitic bullying by gangs who would chase and throw rocks at him. He developed a love of learning and attended City College, New York, then went to the University of Wisconsin to study psychology. At Columbia University, he worked for a while with Alfred Adler (1870–1937), an early colleague of Sigmund Freud's, and the experience persuaded him that he wanted to focus on mental health and human potential.

Maslow set out to discover the sources of personal strength and fulfilment, and examined the drives that motivate people. The most famous aspect of his work is his 'hierarchy of needs', still frequently cited in management psychology, and the concepts of 'self-actualization' (see pages 193–4 and 216–17) and 'peak experiences'.

Maslow and the co-founder of the humanistic school, fellow American Carl Rogers (1902–87), rejected an empirical scientific approach altogether. Instead, they used qualitative and subjective methods such as looking at biographical and autobiographical accounts, conducting open-ended questionnaires, unstructured interviews and observations, and using case studies. One of their aims was to find out from people who had realized their full potential in life (self-actualized) exactly how they had done it. Maslow and Rogers focused on individual experiences, finding richness in the subjectivity that would not have been possible with a more rigorously scientific approach. We will see more of their work in Chapter 6.

A broad approach

Cognitive psychology was the second 20th-century school to reject animal experimentation. Modern cognitive psychology takes a range of approaches, including information-processing, cybernetics, linguistics and neurology in addition to mainstream psychological traditions. Accordingly, although a lot of cognitive psychology research is conducted through laboratory or field experiments with human subjects, some of it also makes extensive use of computer technologies.

EXPERIMENTING ON HUMANS

Experiments with human subjects invariably involve a degree of chaos and subjectivity.

In the past, a popular practice was to tell subjects that they were being tested or observed in one way, while the researcher was actually interested in a different aspect. This meant the subject would pay extra attention to the aspect they believed was being observed, but they would be likely to act more naturally in other regards – including the aspect that was the true subject of the investigation.

In one example, a group of volunteers are invited to sit in a room and answer a written intelligence test. While they're focusing on this, someone steals a wallet from one of their jackets. The volunteers think they are there solely to do the test, but they are in fact being studied to see how they react to the apparent theft.

Social psychology

Social psychology, another 20th-century development, looks at how people behave in groups (and therefore in relation to one another). It grew in influence after World War II, when psychologists became interested in the ways some people behave towards those with greater or lesser power. Some of the most famous studies in psychology belong to this school, including Stanley Milgram's study of obedience (see pages 208–11) and Phil Zimbardo's study of how prisoners and prison guards behave if given free rein (see pages 200–203).

Many social psychology experiments are field experiments, but not all situations can be found or staged in the real world. Zimbardo's experiment, for example, could not have been staged by observing a real prison as the behaviour of guards is constrained by regulations. Clearly, an experiment in a laboratory lacks authenticity, and there are always questions to consider about how far the results can be extended to situations outside the laboratory. However, a field study does not allow the researcher full control of the variables.

An example makes this clearer. In 1968, Irving and Jane Piliavin set out to investigate bystander behaviour in an emergency. The researchers hired actors to board a crowded train on the New York subway and fake a collapse. The researchers were present as observers and studied the responses of passengers. They repeated the experiment with different 'victims' and approaches. Three of the 'victims' were white and one was black, but all dressed alike. Each one either pretended to be drunk, or remained sober and carried a walking stick (implying a disability). These were the variables the researchers could control. They had no control over possible 'confounding variables', such as how many people would be present in the train compartment at the time, and how representative they were of society in general.

The researchers were interested in how quickly and how often help was offered, and in the gender and racial profile of the helpers. They found more men than women helped, and that the drunken victims were helped less frequently than the stick-carrying victims (nearly 50 per cent, compared to 95 per cent). The researchers concluded that in situations such as this, people subconsciously carry out a cost/reward assessment, balancing the cost to themselves of helping (disgust, embarrassment, risk of assault or getting covered in vomit, for example) against the reward they might anticipate (praise, or a clear conscience, for example). They found, counter to other studies, that people's readiness to help in this instance was not affected by the number of passengers in the carriage. Generally, the 'bystander effect' means that people are less likely to help if there are others present, as responsibility is dissipated and it's easier to think 'someone else will do it'.

Pick and mix

From the late 20th century onwards, psychology has not been dominated by any one particular school. Today, it is an eclectic mix of methods that co-exist more or less amicably. As such, it employs a number of experimental methods that have been used in the past, but includes new ones that take advantage of technologies not previously available.

Areas of brain function, for instance, can be investigated using functional MRI (fMRI) scanners that show which parts of the brain are working when a particular stimulus is applied or activity carried out. Brain scans can also be used to compare the structures of different brains. There are, for instance, distinctive characteristics in the brains of psychopaths compared with the brains of non-psychopaths (see panel on page 230) or in the brains of taxi drivers with highly developed navigational knowledge compared with those of a control group made up of people who aren't taxi drivers (see panel below).

Psychology has become increasingly interdisciplinary: more and more studies are in applications of psychology, including therapy, education, management, marketing, sociology, computing, social engineering and political science. It is now sometimes hard to say where psychology begins and ends.

THE ELASTIC BRAIN

In 2000, Eleanor Maguire at University College London used magnetic resonance imaging (MRI) to study the brains of London taxi drivers. She compared scans of their brains with those of men of similar age and profile. She noticed that the taxi drivers had significantly larger posterior hippocampi than those in the control group. This area of the brain is important in navigation and spatial awareness. To qualify as London cabbies, drivers must spend up to four years learning routes through the 25,000 streets of London (a process known as acquiring 'The Knowledge'), so their hippocampi get plenty of exercise. She concluded that this part of the brain can adapt with use, expanding like an exercised muscle. The taxi drivers also had smaller anterior hippocampi than the control group, suggesting they had shrunk to make room for the expansion of the larger posterior hippocampi. Maguire found that the longer the men had worked as taxi drivers, the more marked the difference between their brains and those of the control group. In a follow-up study, she examined brain scans of retired taxi drivers, and found that the size of the larger posterior hippocampus shrank when it was no longer being used extensively. Using an fMRI scanner, she examined the brains of taxi drivers as they played a computer simulation of driving, and found that the hippocampus was active while a driver was thinking about a route. Just as important as discovering the area of the brain used in navigation was her finding that the brain can adapt and grow, even in an adult.

CHAPTER 4
Is knowledge innate or acquired?

*'Language and culture are the frameworks
through which humans experience,
communicate and understand reality.'*
Soviet psychologist Lev Vygotsky (1896–1934)

One of the principal functions of the brain is to know things.
The question – How do we obtain knowledge? – has taxed
philosophers and psychologists for millennia. Whatever the
starting point of our brain at birth, we need to populate it with
knowledge. What is going on in our brain when we learn?

How do we actually 'know' things and store that knowledge? How do we choose what to remember? How do we recall it later? Why do we forget some of it? Why do we remember certain traumatic events, but fail to remember others? And how does this remembering/forgetting affect our lives?

Ways of knowing

DEMONSTRATIVE AND EMPIRICAL KNOWLEDGE

The Scottish philosopher David Hume (1711–76) believed there to be only two valid types of knowledge: 'demonstrative' and 'empirical'. Demonstrative knowledge is produced by imagination and reason, and works by putting together ideas that don't necessarily have any correlation to the real world. Mathematical and other theoretical knowledge fall into this category. For example, the abstract statement that there is an infinite number of different infinities (positive numbers, negative numbers, fractions, and so on) can be deduced through reasoning but cannot be 'experienced'. Empirical knowledge is based on sensory experience, rather than innate ideas or traditions. It prioritizes evidence from the external world in constructing knowledge. Everything else, including all religion and metaphysics, Hume considered to be 'sophistry and illusion'.

Following Hume's model, building knowledge can happen in one of two ways: through our sensory experience of the outside world, or entirely internally. If you see a dog walking down the street, this new knowledge – that there is a dog walking down the street – involves processing information about the world from your senses. It is empirical. However, if you are just thinking about whether you like dogs, you are working with ideas you have formed already and it is a process that is wholly internal to the mind. It is demonstrative.

RATIONALISM VERSUS EMPIRICISM

Philosophers have held different views about the relative reliability of different sources of knowledge. Demonstrative and empirical knowledge relate to two schools of thought that can be traced back to Ancient Greece: 'empiricism' and 'rationalism'. Aristotle championed the empiricist view, believing that the only solid basis for reasoning and knowledge derived from information we can test with our own senses. The opposite – rationalist – view, looks to reasoning to provide knowledge. Plato was a rationalist; he argued that our senses can only perceive reality imperfectly, therefore sense impressions are not a reliable basis for knowledge. He saw reason, instead, as the highest and distinguishing faculty of humankind, and the only way to arrive at secure knowledge.

In the late 16th and early 17th centuries, empiricism and rationalism each had a great spokesman who set the terms for a debate that would develop over the coming centuries. In the empiricist corner was the English philosopher and scientist Francis Bacon (1561–1626), who distrusted reason and believed that the only reliable knowledge was based on observation of the real world. Rationalism was problematic, in his view, because people were prone to adhere to ideas and biases they already had and allow these to colour their perceptions when thinking theoretically. He also observed that people were prone to arguing about the meaning of words rather than the actual nature of phenomena. His attitude, that all valid knowledge can be verified by empirical observation, is one that would later be called 'positivism'.

In the opposing corner, the French philosopher René Descartes championed reason. Unable to trust his perception of the outside world, he decided that if he started with cognition he could incrementally build a body of reliable knowledge without depending on his senses. Descartes' rationalist influence was so great that most European philosophers over the following century set out their stalls answering, supporting or challenging aspects of Cartesian philosophy (so-named in his honour).

PERCEPTION IS REAL, BUT WHAT ABOUT THE PERCEIVED?

Hume, who was one of the most important British empiricists, claimed that all we have to go on in creating knowledge is our perceptions, and we can have no confidence in the existence of anything other than the fact that we have sensory experiences. The question of whether what we perceive actually relates to reality is unanswerable. He was not the only one to think this; the 5th-century Sophists had declared that there is no such thing as certain knowledge. The German philosopher and psychologist Franz Brentano (1838–1917) claimed that while we can be absolutely certain of our perceptions – we can be sure we hear a bell or see a ball, for example – we can't be at all sure that the perception relates to anything in the external world. The fact of hearing or seeing he called internal perception. Sensory perceptions – those which appear to be of the external world – Brentano considered to be capable only of giving us theories, not the facts, about what is 'out there'.

COMMON SENSE

Whether or not Hume rationally believed in the evidence of his senses, his contemporary, the Scottish philosopher Thomas Reid (1710–96), did. Reid said that common sense dictates we all rely on our senses to get through life; for anyone, even Hume, to believe otherwise would lead to them being 'clapped into a madhouse'. Reid didn't believe that we need reason at all in order to interpret the evidence of our senses – we just perceive things directly, with no processing of sensations. As evidence of this, he pointed out that children (and many adults) have no reasoning powers; if a complex train of thought were necessary for them to comprehend their perceptions, they would gain no benefit from their senses and be unable to live effectively.

The great German thinker Immanuel Kant (1724–1804), one of the most influential and important of all philosophers, agreed with Hume on the unreliability of the senses. He referred to the objects 'out there' that constitute external reality as noumena, or 'things-in-themselves'. He agreed that we can know nothing about them with any certainty as they are only mediated through our senses. What we *can* know about are phenomena – the appearances of noumena as they have been modified by sensory perception – and categories of thought. The categories of thought were the significant point of difference between Kant and Hume; there is more about them in Chapter 5.

Sensation and perception

However reliable or unreliable our senses may be as mediators of the outside world (if there is one), they are, as Reid said, all we have to go on. Our psychological interaction with the outside world, and the world of our own physical body, takes place through the processes of sensation and perception. The two are intimately linked but discrete. Sensation is the process of sensing through the physical senses of vision, hearing, touch, and taste and other sensory mechanisms such as feeling pain or heat. Perception is the act of making meaning from that, of understanding the sensory information. When psychologists are not distinguishing between the two processes, they often run the words together in the composite 'sense perception'.

ONE AND THE SAME?

In order for sensation to lead to perception, we must suppose either that the body and mind communicate or that they are one and the same. Suppose you cut your finger. There are different levels of response:

- Your finger bleeds: this is a mechanical response, following the laws of matter and fluid dynamics. It's the same as if you cut through a pipe in which water was pumped.

- You feel pain: this is a shared physical and mental event where the body and mind need to work together. The pain begins as the stimulation of a nerve (a sensation). In the brain, the sensation is interpreted (perceived) as pain.

- You might feel anger, shock, or some other emotion related to having been hurt: this occurs inside the mind through processes of association. It is not produced by the nerves which were stimulated by the cut.

The Greek physician Alcmaeon of Croton (5th century BC) was possibly the first person to dissect the human body for scientific reasons. By tracing the optic nerve from the eye to the brain, either in humans or animals, he discovered the connection between the senses and the brain. He tested the function of the optic nerve by severing it in animals and studying the outcome. He concluded that all perception, thought, memory and understanding were carried out by the brain, even though the source information came from the sensory organs. We agree with Alcmaeon now, although plenty of thinkers between his time and ours have seen the process rather differently.

ALL DOWN TO ATOMS

The Greek scientist-philosopher Democritus (c.460–370BC) was the first to propose an entirely physical means for perception (and everything else). With no recourse to gods, he described impressions in terms of the five physical senses receiving 'atoms' emanating from the physical universe and relaying them to the brain. Here, the mobile 'fire atoms' of

> the brain make copies of the objects. The copies may not
> be accurate, so there can be a mismatch between what we
> perceive and what exists. Democritus is often regarded as
> the father of modern science.

The Ancient Greek philosopher Epicurus (341–270BC) suggested that the psyche is made of very fine matter which is distributed throughout the physical body, so that body and mind are an aggregate. Acts of sensation and perception are possible because the mind is integrated into the body parts, so readily works in sympathy with them. Epicurus was a physical monist.

The Roman philosopher Lucretius (99–55BC) believed the soul to be separate and divided it into a thinking part (*animus*) and a sensing part (*anima*). The thinking part, he said, is located in the chest, but the sensing part is distributed throughout the body. The *animus* can cut itself off from the body, but the *anima* cannot. In cases of strong emotion, both parts are inextricably involved.

For the Stoics, the sympathy between body and psyche was sufficient to prove that the psyche is one and the same thing as the body (see panel below).

> 'No incorporeal interacts with a body, and no body with
> an incorporeal, but one body interacts with another body.
> Now the soul interacts with the body when it is sick and
> being cut, and the body with the soul; thus when the
> soul feels shame and fear the body turns red and pale
> respectively. Therefore, the soul is a body.'
> **Nemesius, Christian philosopher and author of**
> **the treatise De Natura Hominis (c.AD390)**

ON HUMAN UNDERSTANDING

In 1689, the English physician and philosopher John Locke (1632–1704) published an influential book which describes the human mind as a blank slate that is populated with knowledge gained through experience during a person's lifetime. *An Essay Concerning Human Understanding* is one of the main sources of modern empiricist thinking and may have been the first full-length text to tackle aspects of psychology.

Locke set out to challenge the rationalist notion of innate ideas: 'If we will attentively consider newborn children,' he wrote, 'we shall have little reason to think that they bring many ideas into the world with them.' He believed that the mind has just two types of material to work with, asserting that all knowledge comes either directly from sense perceptions or from reflection. Sense perceptions are formulated from the information we receive through our sensory organs, such as our eyes and ears. Reflection, Locke explained, is 'the perception of the operations of our own mind within us, as it is employed about the ideas it has got'. As reflection works on digested earlier perceptions, which in turn also come from sensations, it all comes down to sensations in the end. The interface between the world and the mind is, therefore, perception. We forge knowledge by making associations between ideas – and ideas themselves are formed from perceptions and the sensations they leave behind in the mind. So, sorting out how perceptions are produced is crucial to understanding how we acquire knowledge. (Note that there are two types of 'sensation' here – one is the stimulation of nerves in a sensory organ, and the other is an echo of perception left in the mind, which can be revived for a later perception-by-reflection.)

PERCEPTION AND APPERCEPTION

Gottfried Leibniz (see pages 27–8) was interested in how each perception is made up of infinitely tiny perceptions, or 'petites perceptions', that are not apperceived (consciously reflected upon by the mind). Leibniz gave as an example of a 'petite perception' the experience of listening to the sound of crashing waves. It is, he points out, made up of perceptions of lots of small movements of water, some so tiny that we wouldn't be consciously aware of them if they occurred alone. Yet they combine to make us consciously aware of the sound of the sea, and a sensation cannot be made up from a lot of nothings. For Leibniz, the point at which there is sufficient mass of micro-perceptions to be noticeable is called 'apperception'; therefore, apperception is the point of awareness. There is also a threshold, or 'limen', below which the perceptions we have remain unconscious. Leibniz was possibly the first philosopher to give a clear account of an unconscious mind. His notion of limen was explored experimentally in the psychophysics experiments of the 19th century, and measured as the 'just noticeable difference' by Weber and Fechner (see pages 56–60).

CREATING THE WORLD BY PERCEIVING IT

Alarmed at the way materialism was eroding the domain of God, Bishop George Berkeley (1685–1753) threw out materialist arguments wholesale, along with matter, and adopted a subjective idealist position (that only minds and mental contents exist). He contended that all we have are our sense-perceptions and they are what create the world for us:

> *'All those bodies which compose the mighty frame of the world, have not any subsistence without a mind; that their being is to be perceived or known; that consequently so long as they are not actually perceived by me, or do not exist in my mind, or that of any other created spirit, they must either have no existence at all, or else subsist in the mind of some Eternal Spirit.'*

His conclusion – that things don't exist if they are not being perceived – allocates to the mind all responsibility for keeping the physical universe in existence. To get around the obvious problem that, for instance, the carrots you put in the fridge are there when you look later but apparently didn't exist the moment you shut the fridge door, Berkeley enlists the help of the divine. When no 'created spirit' is keeping an eye on the material world, God takes over: 'When I shut my eyes, the things I saw may still exist; but it must be in another mind.' This extreme, empiricist view asserts that the nature of the world can only be approached through proper speculation and reasoning.

Berkeley's account of perception is important because it shows how complex ideas are put together from multiple sense-perceptions. Berkeley did not deny the existence of physical objects such as trees and mountains, but denied the knowability or existence of matter as a metaphysical substance:

> *'I do not argue against the existence of any one thing that we can apprehend, either by sense or reflection. That the things I see with mine eyes and touch with my hands do exist, really exist, I make not the least question. The only thing whose existence we deny is that which philosophers call matter or corporeal substance. And in doing of this, there is no damage done to the rest of mankind, who, I dare say, will never miss it.'*

We might dispute whether there really is no such thing as a tree, but when Berkeley extends the same principle to abstracts that we perceive, he has a good point. We put together the idea of a tree from our own perception of its size, shape, smell, the feel of the bark, the rustling of the leaves, and so on. According to Berkeley, objective reality is completely dependent upon the minds of the subjects that perceive it.

EXPERIMENTAL WORK ON PERCEPTION

The early experimental work of the 19th century focused on perception and sensation. First Weber and Fechner, and then Wundt, and later the structuralist and functionalist psychologists, all used empirical physical methods to study the thresholds of perception and the possible elements of perception. In Edward Titchener's studies, for example, introspective analysis might reveal that a subject perceived the distinctive taste and smell of a fruit, and its colour, shape, solidity, texture, and weight. Titchener would have classed these as separated sensory experiences that the mind puts together to experience an apple or an orange. Müller's work on the nerves demonstrated that the eyes sensed the colour and the nose the smell of the fruit (see pages 54–5). The brain then translates the information from the eyes into a visual image of, say, something that is orange and round.

Starting to know

There is a big difference between perceiving a pattern of light or sounds and understanding or interpreting it. Information that is sent from the sensory organs to the brain is processed in order to be perceived, but then the brain needs to do more work with it to know what it means, to store it for later, or to act on it. Once the brain has received information from the senses observing an apple or an orange, it does a lot of work to construct and recognize the fruit.

ASSOCIATION

Aristotle believed that the mind – or our 'common sense' – makes links between sensations and events, which are largely based on their appearing close to one another in time or space, or occurring together frequently. The mind also associates things that are similar, and sometimes even things that contrast with one another (such as hot and cold, or sweet and sour). These associations, he asserted, are the basis of knowledge. He believed that common sense is responsible for bringing together all aspects or 'elements' of something to create the idea of it. So, it might bring together colour, smell, shape, texture and taste to produce the idea of an orange, for instance. This association of ideas was accepted for two millennia without much further investigation until David Hume looked at it again in the 18th century.

ASSOCIATIONISM FLOURISHES

The English physician and philosopher David Hartley (1705–57) asserted that if we consistently experience several events or sensations together, our minds store them as a package. Encountering just one of the set then recalls all the others. For Hartley, the key aspect of association was contiguity – that ideas or impressions that were always encountered together 'clumped' in that way. Hartley made the first attempt to give a physical account of how sense impressions became ideas in the mind. He proposed that sense-perceptions produce vibrations in the nerves that travel to the brain and cause corresponding vibrations there. These brain vibrations produce sensations. When the sensation has passed, slight echoes or remnants of the vibrations exist, called (rather prettily) 'vibratiuncles'. These correspond to ideas of sensation, and account for memory. Therefore, complex ideas can coalesce into even more complex ('decomplex') ideas. Hartley's account of how associations form and how mental events correlate to biology remained authoritative for 80 years.

> '*As simple ideas run into complex ones by association,*
> *so complex ideas run into decomplex ones by the same.*'

LAWS OF ASSOCIATION

There are generally considered to be three or four ways in which the mind uses association to build ideas from 'elements'.

1. *The law of contiguity: things that occur close together in space or time are linked by the mind. If you think of a fork, you might also think of a knife to go with it.*
2. *The law of frequency: if two things or events are linked, the association between them will be stronger the more frequently you come across them together. If your grandma always gave you home-baked cakes, you are likely to think of her in association with home-baked cakes.*
3. *The law of similarity: the mind associates similar things. If you find one sock on the floor, you will think about the other matching sock and wonder where it might be.*
4. *The law of contrast: sometimes, seeing or thinking something will trigger thoughts of its opposite. If you think about your best friend at school, you might also recall the class bully you hated.*

The Scottish historian and philosopher James Mill (1773–1836) took Hartley's ideas of association further and made them the foundation of all that the mind can do. For him, all ideas comprised several originally separate simple ideas which were always thought of together; so our comprehension of physical objects is really just a collection of perceptions that can't be separated:

'It is to the great law of association that we trace the formation of ideas of what we call external objects; that

*is, the idea of a certain number of sensations, received
together so frequently that they coalesce, as it were, and
are spoken of under the idea of unity. Hence, what we
call the idea of a tree, the idea of a stone, the idea of a
horse, the idea of a man.'*

Simple ideas associate to make complex ideas, and complex ideas
can be combined to make more complex (duplex) ideas, which
in turn can be combined . . . and so on. But the key point is
the reducibility of everything to basic ideas that were formed
from original perceptions. Associations are stronger or weaker
according to how vivid they are and how frequently the ideas are
encountered together.

'And suddenly the memory returns. The taste was that of
the little crumb of madeleine which on Sunday mornings
at Combray . . . my aunt Léonie used to give me, dipping
it first in her own cup of real or of lime-flower tea . . . And
once I had recognized the taste of the crumb of madeleine
soaked in her decoction of lime-flowers . . . immediately
the old grey house upon the street, where her room was,
rose up like the scenery of a theatre to attach itself to the
little pavilion, opening on to the garden, which had been
built out behind it for my parents (the isolated panel which
until that moment had been all that I could see); and with
the house the town, from morning to night and in all
weathers, the Square where I was sent before luncheon,
the streets along which I used to run errands, the country
roads we took when it was fine . . . in that moment all the
flowers in our garden and in M. Swann's park, and the
water-lilies on the Vivonne and the good folk of the village*

> *and their little dwellings and the parish church and the*
> *whole of Combray and of its surroundings, taking their*
> *proper shapes and growing solid, sprang into being, town*
> *and gardens alike, all from my cup of tea.'*
>
> **Marcel Proust, *Remembrance of Things Past* (1913–27)**

Mill's adherence to the laws of association meant that, according to his philosophy, the mind does nothing creative; it is, as Descartes and Hume held it to be, working like a machine and automatically following a set of rules. It also meant that mental events, like physical events, were entirely predictable; there was no space for individuality, creativity, the spark of genius or free will.

BOOK-BURNING

The Swiss-French philosopher Claude Helvetius (1715–71) was a significant influence on James Mill and on his son, John Stuart. A wealthy tax collector married to a countess, Helvetius defined social welfare as the 'greatest happiness of the greatest number', prefiguring the utilitarianist model championed by the English philosopher Jeremy Bentham (1748–1832). He also supported the notion that each individual was a blank slate (tabula rasa) *at birth, and that we are what our experiences have made us – nothing more.*

He argued there was no such thing as good and evil – the only human motive was self-interest. The logical conclusion of his argument was that if we control the experiences someone has, we can control how their mind will develop. Immediately after the publication of Helvetius' first book, Essays on the Mind *(1758), the Church authorities cited it as proof of his attempt to destroy religion, the monarchy, family, and other sacred bonds. The Sorbonne University condemned the book and had it publicly burned in 1759. A terrified Helvetius was forced to write three retractions.*

PSYCHOLOGY ACCOMPLISHED

James Mill's doctrine of inseparable association described how the mind automatically works with its basic elements – sensations – to produce the mental apparatus we experience as humans. He believed he had successfully constructed a 'physics of the mind' comparable with Newtonian physics and the way in which this line of reasoning explained the universe in terms of elemental matter which irrevocably follows immutable physical laws.

Mill's more famous son, John Stuart (1806–73), took on board his father's thinking, with a slight variation. He argued that the study of human nature (psychology) was a precise science. He said the laws governing this science were not yet properly known (they still aren't), but that not knowing them didn't mean they don't exist. Once they were known, he said, it would be possible to explore and explain how individual personalities develop and to predict how people behave in specific circumstances. Their discovery would at last unravel the mystery of human thought.

The faculty of understanding

Immanuel Kant considered that we cannot have perfect knowledge of the objective truth, as all we can know is filtered through our sensory perceptions. Our innate categories of thought make sense of our perceptions, and where the sense is universally acknowledged we accept it as objective knowledge. Taking issue with David Hume's contention that causation is not real, Kant argued that while we can't prove that an effect follows a particular cause, it seems to us that causation is real; thought categories organize experience in such a way that we see one thing causing another.

FACULTY PSYCHOLOGY

Thomas Reid – who said that Hume would be clapped in a madhouse if he didn't rely on his senses in day-to-day life – was an early proponent of 'faculty psychology'. This states that the mind has many aspects or functions, called faculties, which interact. Reid identified 43 faculties, including reason, consciousness, compassion, memory, judgement, and morality. Kant was also a faculty psychologist.

Hermann von Helmholtz used 'unconscious inference' to explain how the mind made sense of perceptions. He said we use our past experiences to understand what we see – so once we have seen a sufficient number of different chairs, for example, we will be able to recognize a new one when we see it. Our experience of viewing perspective in a three-dimensional world enables us to perceive that an orange is a sphere and not a disc. He experimented with distorting glasses and found that his subjects soon adjusted to them. Helmholtz's conclusion, that past experience builds sensations into perceptions, was an empiricist one. It differed from Kant's view – that categories of thought were innate and began to operate on sensations straight from birth. Helmholtz believed that the mind must first learn how to perceive.

Modern rationalist psychologists favour a Kantian view of structures in the brain, which pattern our thinking. Empiricists favour a view, like that of Helmholtz, which relies on sensory experience, learning and passive laws of association. With an unfamiliar object, we can determine what it is from subtle effects of light and shade, but with a familiar object we draw on past experience to tell us that an orange is spherical but a pancake is a flat circle.

PERCEIVING AND ACTING

The way we act is governed by how we perceive the world (that is, how our brains model it) rather than how it actually is. The Gestalt psychologist Kurt Koffka distinguished between the geographical environment (the physical world around us) and the behavioural environment (our subjective interpretation of it). He told an old German story to illustrate this point:

A man rides across what he believes to be a snowy plain. When he speaks to someone at the end of his journey, he learns that he has in fact just ridden across a frozen lake that could have given way at any moment. When he realizes the danger he was in, the poor man falls down dead from shock.

This behaviour accords not with the environment as it really is but as what the man believed it to be. Had he known the true nature of the surface he was riding on, he would not have taken that route. His subsequent behaviour, in falling down dead, puts his perception of danger into action – he does what he would have expected to do had he known the true nature of his actions.

CHAPTER 5
The building blocks of the psyche

'Let us then suppose the mind to be, as we say, white paper, void of all characters, without any ideas: – How comes it to be furnished? Whence comes it by that vast store which the busy and boundless fancy of man has painted on it with an almost endless variety? To this I answer, in one word, from experience.'
John Locke, *An Essay Concerning Human Understanding* (1690)

If knowledge is built by processing sensory perceptions or from reflection on knowledge already acquired, what is the mind like before any knowledge has entered it? Is it like a vast empty box into which perceptions are chucked? How does the mind organize all this material and construct links between the innumerable elements? Is the mind involved at all, or is it all down to the way the brain is organized?

What do babies know?

Is the infant's mind a blank slate, waiting for knowledge to be inscribed upon it, or are we all born with some innate knowledge? Another position, part-way between these two, has it that we are born with certain structures in place that make it possible for us to organize knowledge as it is acquired. The process of learning populates these structures with knowledge. The first two positions can be traced back to antiquity, while the midway position – the idea of the mind as 'organizer' – is more recent.

Born knowing

Psamtik I and others who conducted the 'forbidden experiments' on children (see pages 43–4) were not alone in believing that humans are born with some innate knowledge. Plato believed that in their pure state our souls have absolute knowledge, but when the soul enters the body its access to that knowledge is cut off. He considered learning to be a process of uncovering innate knowledge rather than of discovery. This view can be called 'nativistic' in that it assumes there to be certain skills or abilities that are native or hard-wired into the human brain at birth.

Much later, Descartes also proposed that some types of knowledge are innate. The most important of these, he claimed, was knowledge of God, which he considered to be common to all people. (He lived in 16th-century France, where to deny the existence of God was to risk being burnt as a heretic.) Other philosophers have suggested that some types of moral knowledge are innate.

Nativism is not restricted to knowledge. It can encompass any kind of inherited natural tendency or trait. The view that humans are innately savage and only kept in check by society, as Thomas Hobbes believed, is nativistic in that it relies on traits already present in the newborn individual. So is the opposite view, held by the French writer and philosopher Jean-Jacques Rousseau (1712–78), that humans are innately noble but corrupted by society. We will examine Rousseau's thinking later (see pages 150 and 173).

KNOWLEDGE REVEALED

Plato supposed that the soul has perfect knowledge of all things and can see clearly if it is not trapped inside the body. Once inside the body, however, 'instead of investigating reality by itself, it is compelled to peer through the bars of its prison'. Knowledge is subsequently revealed through the process of learning. Plato illustrated this concept by referring to an account of how Socrates questioned a slave about geometry. At first, the slave seemed to know nothing of geometry, but as Socrates quizzed him he slowly revealed an understanding. To Plato this was clear proof that the slave had the knowledge innately but could not access it at first. In fact, it is far more likely that the slave was able to work out the answer by way of Socrates' careful prompting.

Gottfried Leibniz expressed a similar idea in the 18th century. His view was that the universe is populated by points of consciousness called monads. He maintained that the super-strength monads of the human mind possessed ideas that existed as potentialities, until experience or sensory perception activated or actualized them. Just as a dark room might contain several objects that can't be seen until a light is turned on so, for Leibniz, the mind contained innate ideas waiting to be uncovered later on.

KNOWLEDGE FROM THE PAST

The French naturalist Jean-Baptiste Lamarck (1744–1829) proposed the theory that evolution occurred through the inheritance of acquired characteristics. Lamarck suggested that, during the course of its life, an organism adapts its physical form and behaviour to suit its environment. (The example often given is of the giraffe stretching up to reach the most succulent leaves and extending its neck in the process.) When the organism reproduces, its offspring inherit these acquired characteristics. Through this process, iterated over hundreds or thousands of generations, species change. The theory enjoyed some popular support before being eclipsed by Charles Darwin's theory of evolution by natural selection.

This theory appealed to the English philosopher and biologist Herbert Spencer (1820–1903), a polymath with an interest in psychology. He took Lamarck's use-inheritance theory and applied it to the mind, positing that the brain is developed or diminished by use or disuse and the resulting changes may be passed on to future generations. This theory suggests that the mind has been gradually improving itself over time. The behaviours and beliefs which work well are reinforced, and those which are not beneficial are not. During the course of one lifetime, reinforced behaviours become habits. Habits that have been developed by parents are passed on to their offspring and with the passage of time begin to appear as instincts, since they are ingrained from birth.

The Swiss psychiatrist Carl Jung's (1875–1961) concept of analytical psychology included the collective unconscious and archetypes. These both relate to supposedly universal and recurring major themes and recall Spencer's theory about human behaviour accreting over the generations. According to Jung, the collective unconscious is a set of mental structures that have been built up over human evolution and experienced by all people in different cultures and times. These archetypes represent:

> '[The] whole spiritual heritage of mankind's evolution, born anew in the brain structure of every individual.'

Jung was also interested in spirituality and his explanation of the collective unconscious sometimes suggests that individuals can discover a form of universal spirit, recalling the panpsychic views of Spinoza and Fechner. Elsewhere he describes simply a universal structure of the mind that predisposes all people to see and understand certain things in certain ways. Jung also saw a kind of enlightenment in achieving individuation – a recognition of one's own unique attributes.

Archetypes are psychic patterns that are equivalent to instincts. They can only be uncovered by comparing the myths, imagery and cultural artefacts of different societies and revealing recurrent patterns in these conscious manifestations of the collective unconscious. Examples of archetypes include figures such as the mother, the hero, the wise old woman or the trickster, and near-universal myths such as the flood and the apocalypse. They are also evident (actualized) in human institutions and celebrations such as marriage or coming-of-age rituals which mark the stages of life.

These theories, from Psamtik and Plato to Jung, suggest innate knowledge – that the infant is born with some knowledge, though perhaps waiting to be uncovered by reason or learning. In Jung's case, we are not aware of the knowledge of archetypes but it is made manifest in our social structures and art (and dreams).

The blank slate

The opposite view to that of the mind populated with innate knowledge is that the mind is an empty page upon which life

The flood (above) and the apocalypse (right) are examples of universal archetypes.

experience and perception will leave their mark. Aristotle was the first to propose this of the infant mind. Around 1,300 years later, the Persian scholar Ibn Sina coined the phrase *tabula rasa* or 'blank slate' for the new, untutored mind: 'Human intellect at birth is like a *tabula rasa*, a pure potentiality that is actualized through education and comes to know.'

The Andalusian polymath Ibn Tufail (*c.*1105–85) wrote an early philosophical and allegorical novel in which he described a young boy, Hayy, who is raised by a gazelle on a desert island. In the absence of any human contact, this feral child discovers ultimate truth through the application of reasoned enquiry. Later on, after coming into contact with civilization, Hayy concludes that although religion and material goods may be useful for the masses, they are a distraction from the truth and should be abandoned by those who seek it. Tufail's novel was translated into Latin in 1671, as *Philosophus Autodidactus*, and into English in 1708. It became a European bestseller and influenced many philosophers, including John Locke and Immanuel Kant.

In his *Essay Concerning Human Understanding*, Locke similarly rejected Descartes' notion of innate ideas, such as knowledge of God and natural morality. If these ideas really were innate, argued Locke, they must be present in every mind – and, clearly, they are

Feral children provide psychologists with a rare and valuable opportunity to consider the role of nurture in knowledge acquisition.

not, since some people don't believe in God, some act immorally, and others (who we might now call psychopaths) don't seem to have a concept of morality at all.

Like Ibn Sina, Locke considered the mind of the newborn infant to be like a sheet of white paper upon which experience wrote the text of knowledge. The operations of the mind, including 'perception, thinking, doubting, believing, reasoning, knowing and willing' forge ideas and knowledge from the sensory perceptions we collect. These actions of the mind are innate, even though no mind-content is innate. The mental processes are part of human nature and don't have to be learned; by combining, comparing and separating parts of them, the mind comes up with increasingly complex notions. It also develops its own rules, so the way in which we respond to or process incoming data varies from one person to another. Locke's model gives each individual considerable freedom and self-determination.

> *'Sense and intuition reach but a very little way. The greatest part of our knowledge depends upon deductions and intermediate ideas: and in those cases where we are fain to substitute assent instead of knowledge, and take propositions for true, without being certain they are so, we have need to find out, examine, and compare the grounds of their probability. In both these cases, the faculty which finds out the means, and rightly applies them, to discover certainty in the one, and probability in the other, is that which we call reason.'*
>
> John Locke, *An Essay Concerning Human Understanding* (1690)

The organizing mind

Between the theory of the blank slate and that of the mind primed with innate, inherited knowledge is the theory that the mind has an organizational structure in place from birth, with innate activities that enable it to interpret incoming information and process it in useful ways.

At the most basic level, we can allow that the mind 'knows' how to do its job. Even Locke concedes this degree of innate ability. After all, it is not much more than the heart 'knowing' how to pump blood.

KITTEN CAROUSEL

Some abilities might seem innate, but on testing they are found to need some sensory input to activate them. In 1963, an experiment on vision carried out by cognitive psychologists R. Held and A. Hein demonstrated that the test subjects only developed true depth perception if provided with sufficient visual or kinetic stimulation.

Held and Hein harnessed a pair of kittens to a carousel for three hours a day. The inside of the carousel was decorated with vertical stripes. One kitten could stand up and move round the carousel by itself; the other was placed in a basket which was rotated by the movement of the first kitten. The first kitten was labelled 'active' and the second 'passive'. The kittens could not see each other, nor could they see their own limbs. As the active kitten walked, both moved in a circle. The kittens had been reared in darkness from birth, then were exposed to the carousel and exercised on it for around six weeks. In this way, they both had identical visual stimuli and moved in the same circuit.

At the end of the trial, the active kitten was able to walk with normal paw placement and had a normal level of depth perception, but the passive kitten had not developed either of

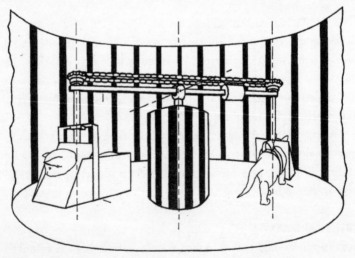

Held and Hein's 'kitten carousel'.

these abilities. Held and Hein concluded that the subjects needed self-directed movement in order to develop perception and visually-guided behaviour.

A later study, in 1980, found that if the passive kittens had interesting things to look at, such as moving toy cars, they did develop depth perception and were better able to walk. The combination of a lack of visual stimulus and absence of self-directed movement prevented the kittens from developing depth perception, but either one on its own was enough. The second study explains why babies strapped to cradleboards in infancy, or born without limbs, are still able to develop depth perception if given sufficient visual stimulation.

In 1961, a study by the Anglo-American anthropologist Colin Turnbull (1924–94) found that humans don't develop depth perception unless they are exposed to things far away and things nearby. Turnbull spent time in the Congo studying the Bambuti people, who live in dense forest. One day, as Turnbull and his assistant, Kenge came to a forest clearing and saw a herd of buffalo grazing miles away, Kenge asked what type of insects they were. When Turnbull explained that they were buffalo, Kenge would not accept it until he drove further and saw them close to. In the forest he had never been able to see more than a few metres away, so had never learned depth perception. With more exposure to distance, Kenge quickly learned the concept of relative size and distance; this demonstrates the plasticity of the brain and how we readily pick up and learn new information.

PRESTRUCTURED

Immanuel Kant also suggested that the mind might have structures in place to store or process particular types of knowledge, including language. Dissatisfied with previous explanations of the relationship between experience and reason, he set out his own theory in the *Critique of Pure Reason* (1781). Kant believed the mind to have 'categories of thought', innate mental structures or concepts that enable it to organize information. These categories give us concepts of time and space and of causation, for example. Simple experience, he maintained, would only ever be enough to show that one event follows another in a chronological sequence, not that one event ever causes another. The categories of thought enable the mind to create meaning even though we are starting just from sense perceptions.

Johannes Müller thought his discovery of the different types of sensory nerve (see pages 54–5) was the physiological equivalent of Kant's categories of thought. He believed he'd found sensory input being worked upon by the nervous system before becoming a thought-object or perception in the conscious mind.

STAGES OF DEVELOPMENT

The Swiss developmental psychologist Jean Piaget (1896–1980) took a distinctly Kantian rationalistic view. He saw the child's mind as possessing schemata which develop slowly over time; initially the child is capable of solely physical interactions with the environment, and develops cognitive abilities later on. The schemata are formed out of building blocks of understanding and can provide understanding of processes or objects. The newborn has some innate, inherited basic schemata which provide reflex actions – the reflex to suckle, for example.

As babies start to learn about their environment, they construct schemata that will help them recognize the same events or objects the next time they encounter them. As their store of experiences grows, they have to adjust their existing schemata and build new ones to accommodate new information. A child who has developed a schema of a cat from a picture book, for instance, will have to adjust it to accommodate the size and furry feel of a cat encountered in real life. If the child encounters a new animal, he or she will need to construct a new schema to explain it. When the child can explain most events and objects, a comfortable state of equilibrium exists. If something new comes along that doesn't fit the existing schemata, disequilibrium results. The child then adjusts his or her schemata to accommodate the new experience, assimilates it, and returns to a state of equilibrium. The ability to form schemata is innate, as is a sort of starter-pack of schemata for essential reflexive and instinctive behaviours.

The British psychologist Frederic Bartlett (1886–1969) further developed the idea of schemata to explain how we process, remember and misremember information. Schemata provide a way of organizing knowledge and ideas, but they can also lead to resistance to new ideas that are hard to slot into our existing categories. Inflexible schemata lead to prejudice and to the distorting of information to fit our expectations.

While Bartlett thought the tendency of the mind to build and populate schemata was innate, the schemata themselves were not. His experimental work included asking people to remember and repeat stories, to complete incomplete stories and to give witness accounts of events. He found that we complete stories and recall events in such ways that they accord with our existing schemata. This makes us unreliable as eye-witnesses, as often we will distort what we see to fit our personal schemata and preconceptions.

THE LANGUAGE INSTINCT
The Canadian cognitive psychologist Steven Pinker (b.1954) considers language to be an instinct in humans and a special adaptation, just like web-building in spiders. He cites the way that deaf children 'babble' with their hands, and believes there is a critical period for language development in children – if they don't learn to speak a

> *language before the cut-off point, they won't learn at all.*
> *This is similar to the cut-off point for vision in cats.*

LANGUAGE: A SPECIAL CASE?

Language seems to set humans apart from other animals. We know of no other species with as wide a range of oral expression as our own, and we know of no human tribe or community that has not developed spoken language. This means that language is a good choice for research into innate/learned behaviours.

In 1660, the French theologian and philosopher Antoine Arnauld (1612–94) and the French grammarian Claude Lancelot (1615–95) published the *Port-Royal Grammar*. In it they argue that grammar is a set of mental processes that are universal, so grammar is innate. A modern champion of this view is the American scientist and philosopher Noam Chomsky (b.1928) who says that children have an innate ability to learn a spoken language. The language they learn depends on the community in which they live, but the basic structures of all languages are universal. Learning a language is simply a matter of populating with content a structure that already exists in the mind. Chomsky maintains that language, with its very complex grammatical structure, is too difficult for a child to pick up by imitation alone.

The idea that there is a universal structure or a natural organizing principle for language is supported by linguistic studies and by various 'experiments of nature'. These are naturally occurring situations that give scientists the opportunity to make observations as though they were carrying out field experiments.

The 'forbidden experiment' with children (see pages 43–4) would no longer be allowed. But there have been various instances of non-speaking parents, deaf or mute, raising children who are capable of language. Many of them learn a signing language used by their parents, but some are brought up without it. Of these, many develop their own way of communicating, called 'homesign', based on signs and gestures. Homesign languages were studied by American psychologists Susan Goldin-Meadow (b.1949) and Heidi Feldman in the 1970s.

THE WAR OF THE GHOSTS

Frederic Bartlett demonstrated the impact of schemata on memory and story-telling by telling his students a traditional North American Indian tale.

One night two young men from Egulac went down to the river to hunt seals from their canoes. While they were there, it became foggy and calm. When they heard war-cries, they thought: 'Maybe this is a war-party.' They escaped to the shore and hid behind a log. Canoes started to approach them along the river; they heard the noise of paddles and one canoe came right up to them. There were five men in it, and they said:

'What do you think? We wish to take you along. We are going up the river to make war on the people.'

One of the two young men said, 'I have no arrows.'

'Arrows are in the canoe,' the visitors said.

'I will not go along,' said the young man, 'I might be killed. My relatives do not know where I have gone. But you,' he said, turning to the other, 'may go with them.'

So the second young man went off in the strange canoe, and the other returned home.

The warriors went on upriver to a town on the other side of Kalama. The townspeople came down to the water and began to fight; many were killed. Presently the young man heard one of the warriors say, 'Quick, let us go home: that Indian has been hit.' At this, the young man thought: 'Oh, they are ghosts.' He did not feel sick, but the warriors said that he had been shot.

So the canoes went back to Egulac and the young man went ashore to his house and made a fire. He told everybody his story, and said: 'Behold I accompanied the ghosts, and we went to fight. Many of our fellows were killed, and many of those who attacked us were killed. They said I was hit, and I did not feel sick.'

Then he grew quiet. When the sun rose, he fell to the ground and something black came out of his mouth. His face became contorted. The people jumped up and cried. He was dead.

Bartlett had his students retell the tale several times over a year, to see how their existing schemata affected their recall. They all thought they were retelling it accurately, but made changes such as:

- *missing out information that was unfamiliar to their lives and situations*
- *changing details, order and emphasis to match what seemed important to them.*

Bartlett concluded that memories are not copies of experience, but rather 'reconstructions'.

They found that homesign systems, although developed independently by isolated children or groups, share grammatical structures. This showed that language does not need to be spoken and that signing develops along the same lines as spoken language with, for instance, word order denoting the function of a word. The conclusion is significant: the basic 'rules' of language – whether verbal or non-verbal – are innate, and even when developed independently reproduce common functions and structures.

Instinctive behaviours

Whether or not we regard the newborn mind as a blank slate, there are undoubtedly some activities we all share. These are reflexive and instinctive behaviours. They don't require knowledge or thinking – they happen automatically. Even Locke would have to admit that the newborn suckles without being taught how to do so.

REFLEXES

A reflex action is a simple, automatic, unlearned response to a stimulus. If you pick up something unexpectedly hot, you will drop it immediately. The instinct that makes you do this is called the withdrawal reflex, and is an example of a reflex arc. When you accidentally touch something very hot, signals from nociceptors (which detect tissue damage) travel to the spinal cord, where they connect with motor nerves; these trigger an automatic response – withdrawing from the source of heat. The signal from the nociceptors also travels to the brain for interpretation, where it is perceived as pain. The reflex movement can start before the pain is perceived.

In the newborn infant, the Moro reflex makes the baby spread out and then pull in his or her arms rapidly. It is a response to a sudden loss of support and may be a survival instinct to help the infant cling to its mother. It is considered to be the only innate (unlearned) fear reflex. Other reflexes of the

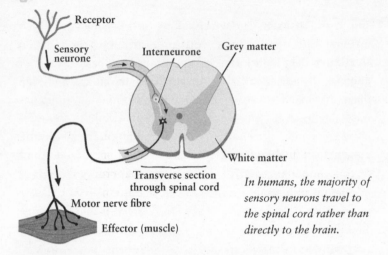

In humans, the majority of sensory neurons travel to the spinal cord rather than directly to the brain.

newborn include the grasping reflex (the fingers curl around an object placed against the palm of the hand) and the rooting and sucking impulses that lead the baby to feed without instruction, demonstration or experience.

PREJUDICES AND STEREOTYPES

In 1947, the American psychologists Gordon Allport (1897–1967) and Leo Postman (1918–2004) carried out a study using a picture of a white man threatening a black man with a razor. Asked to recall and describe the picture they had seen, participants tended to say that the black man was holding the razor. This incorrect recall demonstrates that memory is an active (and unreliable) process and can be changed to 'fit in' with each person's schemata.

FROM REFLEX TO VOLITION

David Hartley outlined the pattern of the child's development from unwilled reflex to voluntary, willed action and through to automatic (but willed) action. To start with, he claimed, we have involuntary behaviours, such as the infant's grasping reflex. As children develop they learn to grasp deliberately and specifically. Babies go from instinctively grasping things to choosing which things to grasp. At this point, the action has become voluntary. Associations, built up from experience, lead a child to choose to grasp something pleasurable – a toy, for instance. Eventually, the action of grasping becomes automatic, so we don't need to think or concentrate to grasp, we just do it when appropriate.

An instinct produces a 'fixed action pattern' (FAP). This is more complex than a reflex, which generally produces a single action. Newly hatched turtles instinctively head to the sea, for instance, and hibernating animals instinctively find and sometimes prepare a suitable place as the day length changes and the temperature drops.

It is generally impossible to suppress a reflex action, but some instincts can be suppressed. Higher animals, such as humans, can often learn the point that triggers an instinctive action and then decide not to carry it out. The fact that it is involuntary initially doesn't mean that it is not susceptible to volition once consciousness is applied. (There are different definitions, though: in 1961, American social psychologists Robert Birney and Richard Teevan claimed an instinct must be irresistible to count as an instinct.)

BEHAVIOURS YOU DON'T HAVE TO LEARN

Instincts were first described by the French naturalist Jean-Henri Casimir Fabre (1823–1915), whose pioneering work with insects established the field of entomology. In one of his more famous experiments, he demonstrated the power of instinct by arranging pine processionary caterpillars around the rim of a circular bowl. As each caterpillar always follows the one in front, they crawled unceasingly around the bowl for seven days.

The first person rigorously to apply instincts to human behaviour was Wilhelm Wundt, who described any repeated behaviour as an instinct. He listed several thousand human instincts. Not long after, Freud suggested that behaviour in response to a natural drive – such as hunger or the impulse to reproduce – was instinctive. By the 20th century, far fewer instinctive behaviours were being assigned to humans. The rise of the behaviourist school of psychology placed much more emphasis on behaviour learned during an individual's lifetime.

LORENZ'S GOSLINGS

The Austrian zoologist Konrad Lorenz (1903–89) was interested in the behaviour of birds. In a series of famous experiments, he exploited the natural instinct of greylag goslings to 'imprint' on a parent figure as soon as they hatch. Normally, this would be the mother bird. The chicks then follow the parent automatically with no further urging. Lorenz was able to show that the goslings would imprint on any nearby object – it didn't have to be a parent. He successfully imprinted goslings to follow his own boots, and they would then follow anyone who was wearing those boots. This combined the generalized instinct to imprint with an element of individual learning. In terms of the mind's structure, the activity – imprinting – is innate, but the thing-imprinted-on comes from the environment.

Classical conditioning

With conditioning, we step outside the realm of innate behaviours and into learning. Although they are repeated responses to the same stimulus, conditioned responses are learned responses. The most famous example is that of the drooling dog experiment carried out by Ivan Pavlov (see page 87). The scientist's name has been adopted to describe this type of classical conditioning – the Pavlovian response.

Pavlovian conditioning begins with a naturally linked stimulus and response pair: the unconditioned stimulus (US) and the unconditioned response (UR). In Pavlov's experiment, the US was the smell or taste of dog food and the UR was salivation. The experimenter links a biologically neutral stimulus, in this case a sound, such as a bell ringing, with the UR. This link is called the conditioned stimulus (CS) because its effects depend on its association with food. Pavlov's dogs came to associate the sound with the taste or smell of meat. The CS then becomes linked with a conditioned response (CR) which is often (but not always) similar or identical to the UR. Pavlov found that the composition of the saliva that the dogs produced in response to the CS was different from that produced in response to the US.

SURPRISE! OR NOT

More recent work on Pavlovian conditioning by the American experimental psychologist Robert Rescorla (b.1940) has shown that the CS (the ringing bell) does not just come to stand for or replace the US (the smell or taste of meat). Rather, the organism (the dog) learns how the ringing of the bell fits into its environment, including its predictive association with the smell or taste of the meat. The complexity of the relationship became apparent when it was shown that if the bell was rung at other times (as well as before or in conjunction with the smell or taste of meat) it did not produce a conditioned response. This showed that the animal's learned ability to predict is crucial to conditioning.

Conditioning is, effectively, the removal of surprise from the experience. As the dog learns that the ringing bell is predictive of the smell or taste of meat, the surprise element of the unconditioned stimulus is reduced.

Conditioned behaviour can be extinguished if the conditioned stimulus is presented repeatedly without the associated unconditioned stimulus. But it can be recovered if the two are associated again (re-learning the link is quicker than the original learning of it), or it can recur spontaneously after an interval with no exposure to the conditioned stimulus.

BEHAVIOUR AND ASSOCIATIONS

When Pavlov discovered the link between conditioned stimulus and a conditioned response, he believed he had discovered the physiological mechanism which lay behind associations, and felt it was unnecessary to look any further to discover how ideas become associated with one another.

LEARNING = PROGRAMMING

The behaviourist John B. Watson (see pages 88–9) was greatly influenced by Pavlov's work. He was convinced that classical conditioning could account for all learning and behaviour, including language. In putting forward his behaviourist model in 1913, he claimed that human character could be entirely determined by careful manipulation of stimulus and response:

'Give me a dozen healthy infants, well-formed, and my own specified world to bring them up in and I'll guarantee to take any one at random and train him to become any

type of specialist I might select – doctor, lawyer, artist, merchant-chief and, yes, even beggar-man and thief – regardless of his talents, penchants, tendencies, abilities, vocations and the race of his ancestors.'

In Watson's model, heredity counts for nothing and environment is everything. Furthermore, personality is entirely determined, leaving no space for free will or even consciousness. Watson was uncompromising in his assertion that behaviour is all we have. That left him without mental structures or schemata to explain how we learn, which is simply a matter of linking a stimulus with a corresponding behaviour and reinforcing the link until it is stable.

CONDITIONED FEAR

Although impressed by Pavlov's work with dogs, Watson needed to demonstrate that it applied also to humans. He did this through the notorious and unethical 'Little Albert' experiment. In 1919, John Watson and Rosalie Rayner, his co-researcher at Johns Hopkins University, selected a nine-month-old infant, referred to as 'Albert', from a nursery. They began by exposing Albert to a range of harmless objects and animals, including a white laboratory rat. He showed no fear or adverse response to any of them – but that was about to change. Next, Watson introducd a stimulus, making a frightening noise by striking a piece of metal with a hammer when Albert touched the rat. The boy cried and showed fear. Watson did this repeatedly until Albert cried and tried to escape when he saw the rat. Albert also became afraid of other furry white objects including a rabbit, a fur coat and a fake beard.

Albert was about one year old at the end of the experiment. Though Watson had discussed plans to remove the child's conditioned fears, he had no time to do so. It's therefore likely that the child's fear of furry things continued after the experiment. Apart from the ethical concerns about the damaging effect upon its subject of such an experiment, critics have complained that as Watson and Rayner used just one test subject, it was impossible to make a fair assessment of the results. Another criticism was that they relied only upon their subjective judgements as a means of recording Albert's responses. Tragically, Albert died at the age of six from hydrocephalus, which he'd had since birth.

CONDITIONING AS THERAPY

In 1924, soon after Watson's Little Albert experiment, the American developmental psychologist Mary Cover Jones (1897–1987) used classical conditioning therapeutically. She worked with a three-year-old boy called Peter, who demonstrated a fear of white rabbits. Over a period of time, she gradually exposed Peter to the rabbit, slowly bringing the two closer together until the child could eventually play happily with the rabbit and even let it nibble his fingers. Other children, who were not afraid of the rabbit, were present in the room, modelling normal responses to the animal. This type of behaviour therapy is still used to treat phobias.

Operant conditioning

Classical conditioning works by training a subject to associate a stimulus with a response, so they learn a behaviour through a process of association. Another type of conditioning starts from the behaviour and works backwards.

Scottish philosopher and educationalist Alexander Bain (1818–1903) is often described as the first British psychologist. He adopted a rigorously scientific approach, seeking to find facts from observation. He classed behaviour as both reflexive and spontaneous. A reflex is automatically elicited by a stimulus: if something splashes in your eye, for example, a reflex action will close the eye. Spontaneous behaviour is initially random, but behaviours that produce a favourable response are remembered and reinforced. Bain was describing learning by trial and error, or 'spontaneous behavioural learning', the process B. F. Skinner would later call 'operant conditioning':

> *'The constant habit of regarding with dread the consequences of violating any of the rules, simulates a moral sentiment, on a subject unconnected with morality properly so called.'*
>
> Alexander Bain

THE CAT IN THE BOX

The early behavioural psychologist Edward Thorndike (1874–1949) laid the groundwork for many later studies of learning. He used animals, often cats, for his work. Thorndike devised a mechanism he called a puzzle box that could be opened from the inside by pressing a lever. The cat was put inside the box, and a scrap of fish was placed outside to encourage the cat to escape. As the cat explored its environment, it eventually stumbled on the lever that opened the box, so then it could reach the fish. Thorndike would put the same cat back in the box several times and record how long it took the cat to use the lever each time. He discovered that the time decreased consistently.

Thorndike formulated the 'law of effect', which states that any behaviour that is followed by pleasant consequences is likely to be repeated, while any behaviour followed by unpleasant consequences is likely to stop. If you pick up a wasp and it stings you, you won't pick up another wasp. If you eat a strawberry and it's tasty, you will probably want to try another. The strength of the conditioning effect depends on the intensity of the response. This simple law, which looks self-evident, would form the basis of behaviourism, one of the most significant movements in 20th century psychology.

ASSOCIATIONISM AND REINFORCEMENT

The associationist model states that we form associations between elements on the basis of them occurring together (contiguity), or being often in close proximity in time or space (frequency), or sometimes because they are markedly dissimilar (contrast). With Thorndike's puzzle boxes, a new model of learning emerged, known as reinforcement. This applied especially to behaviour. A behaviour is reinforced if the response to it is positive, and this encourages repetition of the behaviour.

ELECTRIFIED RATS

The Polish neurophysiologist Jerzy Konorski (1903–73) was the first person thoroughly to explore operant conditioning. He had worked with Pavlov for two years, and originally called the discovery 'Type II' or secondary conditioned reflexes. But the name most often linked with operant conditioning is that of B. F. Skinner, who was living and working in the USA while Konorski was struggling in Stalin's Soviet Union, outside the mainstream world of psychology. Skinner took an extreme position, which he called 'radical behaviourism', and was uncompromising in his assertion that, firstly, we have no free will and, secondly, mental events are of no real consequence in psychology. He has been called the most influential psychologist of the 20th century.

Like Thorndike, Skinner used boxes to test response and learning in animals, and then applied his findings to human psychology. The Skinner box, as his adaptation is known, has a lever that can be used to dispense food, but also interacts with other stimuli – a light, an electrified floor grid, and a speaker. Skinner's favourite test animal was the white rat, but he also experimented on pigeons. When the animals pressed the lever, he tested their responses to the different outcomes – these could be positive, negative or neutral – and he worked with both rewards and punishments.

When the rat knocked the lever and received a food pellet, the behaviour was positively reinforced; because it was rewarded, the rat was likely to repeat it. On other occasions, a mild electric current was run through the floor of the box, making it uncomfortable for the rat. The animal discovered that by knocking the lever it could switch off the current. Its behaviour was negatively reinforced – it removed an unpleasant stimulus – so the rat was likely to repeat it. If Skinner turned on a light in the box, shortly before running the electric current through the floor, the rats learned that the light was a signal and went immediately to the lever to disable the current before it started.

GAMBLING PIGEONS

In 2013, a team of researchers led by Jennifer Laude discovered that some pigeons like to gamble. The pigeons were offered two keys to peck. One key gave ten food pellets for 20 per cent of the time, but nothing for the remaining 80 per cent of the time, while the other key rewarded the pigeon with three pellets 100 per cent of the time. The researchers discovered that some pigeons preferred the big-jackpot strategy. Further tests showed these pigeons to be impulsive – they were unable to delay gratification. To test impulsivity in a pigeon, the researchers again offered two keys, both of which paid out every time. One produced a large pay-out after a delay of 20 seconds. The other produced a small pay-out immediately. The more impulsive pigeons preferred pecking the key that gave them a little pay-out immediately over waiting 20 seconds for the larger pay-out. Compulsive gambling in humans follows a similar pattern and is now recognized as an impulse disorder.

Skinner explored different ways of using reinforcement with both rewards and punishments, with fixed or variable intervals between reinforcement, and fixed or variable ratios of reinforced to non-reinforced behaviour. Interval-based reinforcement schedules lead to slower behaviour – the number of acts doesn't affect the reinforcement, which comes only with passing time. This means the subject receives the reinforcement just by waiting. Ratio-based reinforcement schedules produce faster response rates; since the subject doesn't know when to expect the reinforcement, they will try repeatedly, even frantically, to elicit it.

PIGEON MISSILES
Since boyhood, Skinner had enjoyed making odd devices. During World War II he designed a pigeon-guided missile. The nose-cone of the missile was divided into three compartments, with a space for a pigeon in each. The trained pigeons would guide the missile by pecking at a picture of the target on a screen. If the pecks (and target) were not central on the screen, the pecking caused the missile's path to be adjusted. Although it was successful when demonstrated, and $25,000 of funding was allocated to it, the project was cancelled in 1944 and the funds directed to more conventional research.

Back to the mind

The behaviourist school regarded learning as a process of physical programming. Other psychologists, particularly followers of the Gestalt model, rejected the behaviourists' attempt to separate stimulus and programmed response, preferring instead to see a pattern of learning that fitted into the whole mental state of the organism.

While Wolfgang Köhler was possibly working as a spy on Tenerife, he was also experimenting on chimpanzees and chickens to discover more about learning. He watched the chimpanzees work out how to use tools such as boxes, poles and sticks to reach food that was otherwise unobtainable. He concluded that sophisticated animals learn by a system of cognitive trial and error, considering possible solutions and trying them out mentally before putting the most feasible into practice. The point at which the animal seems to have the answer to the problem is the moment of insight.

A problem is therefore either solved or unsolved, with no states in between. According to Köhler, when insightful learning occurs, the learned result is much more mentally 'sticky' than the result of rote learning or behavioural trial and error. The insight derives from the individual's own combination of previous experiences, memories and configuration of mental fields, and it comes about as an understanding of the structure of the problem and the situation.

MAKING COMPARISONS

In another experiment, Köhler presented chickens with pieces of white and grey paper upon which he had sprinkled grain. He shooed away the chickens that wanted to eat the grain from the white paper, but allowed the chickens to eat from the grey paper. Eventually, the chickens learned that they could eat from the grey sheet but not the white sheet and approached the grey sheet out of preference. Köhler had successfully taught or 'conditioned' the chickens.

He then repeated the experiment with grey and black paper. A standard behaviourist model would suggest that the chickens would immediately go to the grey paper, as they had been conditioned to choose that shade. But the chickens went straight to the black paper. Köhler concluded that the chickens had learned a comparison-based model – they knew that the darker of the two papers held the permitted grain. The chickens, having learned a principle, applied the same principle ('eat from darker paper') to a similar situation, a process Köhler called 'transposition'.

INSIGHTS INTO INSIGHT

Max Wertheimer discovered that people learn better if they have insight. For each individual, this comes in different ways and from different sources. Consequently, there is not necessarily a single best way to learn – it is highly individual. Memory and learning both work through a system of traces laid down by repeated personal experiences. Our recognition of, say, a cat is dependent upon and informed by all our previous encounters with cats and the memories we have of them. We each have our own concept (or schema) of 'catness' that adapts or is reinforced as time passes and we come across more cats. Although some features will be shared – the general physical appearance of a cat, for instance – other aspects will have been drawn from personal experience of individual cats. Someone who remembers a beloved pet from childhood will have a different impression of cats than someone whose predominant memory is of being attacked by a vicious cat.

TOWARDS SOME THEORIES OF LEARNING

The Gestalt psychologists had considerable influence on the cognitive school, which put discovering knowledge and constructing meaning at the centre of learning. Learning, after all, is not only about finding a way out of a maze or beginning to speak and walk – it is also about education. Cognitive psychologists saw learning as highly personal, depending on the individual's existing stock of associations and experiences, as exemplified in Bartlett and Piaget's schemata and Piaget's account of the stages of cognitive development in children (see pages 150–1).

Even the behaviourist Edward Thorndike recognized that an individual's prior knowledge and patterns of association – or the number of stimulus-response patterns they have – can be relevant to future learning. Thorndike was the first to suggest that learning the Classics did not necessarily help with other areas of learning. In general, being adept at one subject did not help with learning another unless the subjects were directly related and there were transferable skills or knowledge. Thorndike advocated learning in chunks and making the material relevant to the learner's own conditions and life.

'If, by a miracle of mechanical ingenuity, a book could be so arranged that only to him who had done what was directed on page one would page two become visible, and so on, much that now requires personal instruction could be managed by print.'

Edward Thorndike (1912)

John Dewey, an educationalist as well as a psychologist, stressed the importance of making learning relevant to the student. He also said that learning materials should encourage original thought and problem solving. Piaget argued that education should take account of the child's cognitive development, something which he divided into clear stages. This was not entirely new. In *Émile, or On Education* (1762), the first text on the philosophy of education in the Western world, Jean-Jacques Rousseau suggested that religious education should be saved for adolescence as before this time the mind is too immature to understand the implications of religious knowledge and beliefs. What is produced in a young child is only the parroting of religious doctrine, not true understanding or faith.

Rousseau proposed that education is best achieved though exploration and discovery. He gave the example of a father taking his boy out to fly a kite. The father showed his son the shadow of the kite on the ground and asked him to work out its position in the sky from the shadow. Although the boy has never been taught how to do this, he is able to work out the answer correctly. The child, Rousseau suggested, is able to learn through inference and an understanding of the physical world. A direct line can be drawn from Rousseau to modern child-centred psychological models, taking in John Dewey and the Italian physician and educator Maria Montessori (1870–1952) along the way.

> 'The noblest work in education is to make a reasoning man, and we expect to train a young child by making him reason! This is beginning at the end; this is making an instrument of a result. If children understood how to reason they would not need to be educated.'
>
> **Jean-Jacques Rousseau (1762)**

Piaget believed that cognitive development was led by biology – attempts to get a child to learn tasks that are beyond his or her stage of development are doomed to fail. Like Rousseau, Piaget recommended learning that is active and based on discovery. The Plowden Report (1967), which set out the scheme for primary school education in the UK, was based on Piaget's research in the 1950s.

> ### PIAGET'S STAGES OF DEVELOPMENT
> *0–2 years: sensorimotor stage – learns object permanence*
> *2–7 years: preoperational stage – child is egocentric*
> *7–10 years: concrete operational stage – understands conservation of number and volume*
> *11+ years: formal operational stage – can manipulate ideas and engage in abstract reasoning*

COMPUTER MEMORY, HUMAN MEMORY

From the 1960s, cognitive approaches were based on the model of the computer as an information-processing mechanism. The concept of schemata fitted well with the structure of computer data storage and manipulation. In 1968, the American psychologists Richard Atkinson (b.1929) and Richard Shiffrin (b.1942) invented the Atkinson–Shiffrin model of memory for the human mind. It is remarkably similar to the way in which a computer handles the input and storage of data. The model suggested three components:

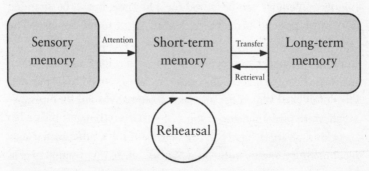

A diagram of the Atkinson–Shiffrin memory model.

- Sensory buffers: each sense organ has a buffer which receives sensory information but does not process it. The information is stored for a short while, and passed to short-term memory only if attention is paid to it.
- Short-term or working memory: this receives and holds input from the sensory buffers, or information retrieved from long-term memory.
- Long-term memory: this stores information indefinitely.

The sensory buffer is part of a filtering process that allows us to select which stimuli we will pay attention to. We might take in an entire visual scene but only pay attention to something relevant, such as a threat, an item we're searching for or a person we know.

We can, according to the American cognitive psychologist George Miller (1920–2012), keep between five and nine items in our short-term memory. He derived this range, fixing on the middle figure of seven, in 1956, from task-based tests on subjects.

Information in short-term memory decays and is forgotten after about 18–20 seconds unless it is rehearsed – in other words, unless attention is continuously or repetitively paid to it. Information in long-term memory can be stored for a lifetime, but to be attended to it must first be brought back into short-term memory. The capacity to store information in long-term memory appears to be limitless – we never stop being able to learn things. In some cases, memories become inaccessible, but they are assumed to be present. Most of us can't remember incidents from babyhood, for example, but they are probably stored somewhere in the brain.

Although there have been criticisms of the model since it was developed, it remains influential. Miller wrote the original article in a spirit of good humour, saying that he felt 'persecuted by an

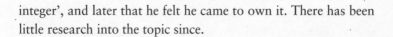

integer', and later that he felt he came to own it. There has been little research into the topic since.

Psychobiology explains it all

Psychobiology attempts to explain the workings of the mind in terms of the physiology of the brain – chemical processes, the firing of neurons, and the organ's physical structure.

The Canadian psychologist Donald Hebb (1904–85) set out to discover the biological processes behind association, but he soon found that nothing in the biology of the brain supported 'associationism'. Instead, he found that a new perception or a shift in attention fires a package of neurons, which he called a 'cell assembly'. For example, Hebb explained how in a child the sound of footsteps triggers a cell assembly that forms a package of perception. The next time the child hears footsteps, the same assembly is excited. If the footsteps are followed by the appearance of a parent, another cell assembly is involved in seeing the parent. The activity of a cell assembly continues for a little while, something he called reverberating neural activity. This means that if another cell assembly was activated in a very short time the two can become linked. A string of cell assemblies connected in this way he called a 'phase sequence'.

> '*When an axon of cell A is near enough to excite cell B and repeatedly or persistently takes part in firing it, some growth process or metabolic change takes place in one or both cells such that A's efficiency, as one of the cells firing B, is increased.*'
> **Donald Hebb,** *The Organization of Behavior* (1949)

The child who hears footsteps and then sees a parent approach will form a phase sequence in which the first perception (the footsteps) automatically calls up the second before it has happened, so the child anticipates the arrival of the parent (and perhaps becomes excited). The cell assemblies and phase sequences can be reactivated either by a genuine external perception (hearing footsteps, in the case of the child) or by an idea. This enables us to conjure up, for instance, the image of a cow when there is no cow in sight – the perceptions that form our idea of a cow are already linked together. The baby, according to Hebb, learns in an 'associationist' way, putting together neural connections to make cell assemblies and phase sequences. The adult, who has already made enough of these to recognize and interpret the environment, learns in a different way, largely by rearranging existing assemblies and phases.

NEURON PRIMER

In 1906, the Italian physician and scientist Camillo Golgi (1843–1926) and the Spanish neuroscientist Santiago Ramón y Cajal (1852–1934) shared the Nobel Prize in Physiology or Medicine for their discovery of neurons. Neurons are nerve cells which carry information as electrical and chemical signals to, from and within the central nervous system (CNS). Sensory neurons carry information about the environment (vision, sound, touch, and so on) from the sense organs to the CNS. Motor neurons carry signals from the CNS to the muscles to control movement. Within the CNS, interneurons connect to one another within the spinal cord and brain to carry and process information.

There are many different types of neuron, but typically they consist of a cell body, an axon (an extension of the cell body, which can be up to a metre long in humans) and dendrites, which are branching ends of the axon. There can be hundreds of dendrites, allowing one neuron to connect with many others. Connections between neurons occur at synapses – tiny gaps at which chemicals carry a signal from one side to the other. The human brain has around 86 billion neurons and perhaps a thousand times as many synapses. The model of neural networks has been copied from the brain to be applied to the design of computer systems.

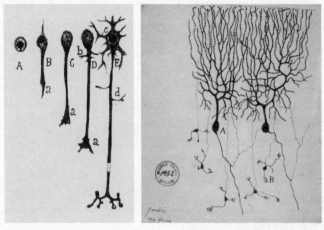

Santiago Ramón y Cajal's sketches of neurons in a pigeon's brain.

CHAPTER 6
Defining the self

*'The self is our life's goal, for it is the
completest expression of the fateful
combination we call individuality.'*
Carl Jung (1875–1961)

What makes one person different from another? Where
do our personalities come from, in psychological or other
aspects? We actually aren't all the same? Defining our
essential identity and identifying its source has preoccupied
people for millennia.

Nature v. nurture

A central, unresolved question in psychology asks how much of our personality, abilities and behaviour can be accounted for by nature (heredity) and how much can be accounted for by nurture (the manner and environment in which we are brought up). Since the time of John Locke, the *tabula rasa* model has been closely associated with the 'nurture' side of the debate, since if nothing is in the mind to start with, the child's carers have complete control over how he or she develops.

Both nature and nurture can be recruited to support a highly deterministic view of personality and fate. According to the 'nature' argument, you could be born with criminal tendencies that are a product of your genetic makeup and compel you to do bad things. According to the 'nurture' argument, you might be raised in a criminal environment that causes you to develop an internal compulsion to do bad things. Studies using twins or adopted children have often been used to try to establish the level of influence that biology and upbringing have on the individual (see pages 169–70).

Free will and determinism

Can we resist hereditary or environmental influences through the agency of free will? The humanistic approach to psychology believes we can – it holds that we make our own choices in life and are each responsible for our own actions. Determinism holds that free will is an illusion and our behaviour is governed by internal or external forces over which we have no control. The behaviourist approach (also known as 'hard determinism') suggests that a person who commits a crime has no real choice in the matter. He or she is driven to it by environmental and genetic conditions and by their personal history. A softer deterministic approach states that the person has a choice, but is constrained by external or internal factors. The issue is further complicated when we consider that any desire or urge to resist the influence of genetics or environment is itself an aspect of character, and therefore a product of genetics or the environment.

Whether we have any control over who we are is an important question, not just for theoretical psychology but for practical applications such as law and education. If someone inherits a gene for psychopathy, are they responsible for their psychopathic actions? If someone's mental makeup has been forged in an environment of abuse, does it predispose them to become an abuser, in the same way that someone brought up in a religious environment is likely to become devout? Or can people look beyond their immediate environment and circumstances and reject their conditioning?

Star-crossed

For thousands of years, people around the world believed our personalities were determined or influenced by the alignment of the heavenly bodies. Natal astrology – casting horoscopes depending on birth date – began around the 6th century BC, with the earliest surviving horoscope dating from 410BC. Central to natal astrology is the belief that the position of the planets and stars at a person's birth can be used as a predictor of their personality and even of events that will occur during their life. Some people still believe this. Unsurprisingly, there is no proven correlation between personality and the position of the Earth in relation to the stars. Even so, astrology provided one of the earliest attempts at explaining personality.

THE RISE, FALL AND RISE AGAIN OF ASTROLOGY

Astrology developed independently in many cultures around the world, including Babylonia, India, China and Mesoamerica. The Babylonian tradition was continued in Egypt and Greece and was carried from there to Rome. After the fall of the Roman Empire, it suffered a decline in Europe but prospered in the Arab world. There was a resurgence in Europe during the Middle Ages when translations of Greek and Arab texts became available, and physicians were expected to check the astrological conditions before starting or recommending a course of treatment for their patients. Even some of the great Renaissance scientists and stargazers, such as the Danish astronomer Tycho Brahe (1546–1601), the Italian polymath Galileo Galilei (1564–1642) and the German mathematician Johannes Kepler (1571–1630), were practising astrologers. They did not necessarily believe in astrology, but it was a useful source of income.

However, with the discovery of comets and the confirmed appearance of new stars, the premise of astrology was thoroughly undermined. After a few attempts to shore it up, it was pretty well abandoned as a science by the 18th century. Its modern reappearance dates from a British national newspaper, the *Daily Express*, casting a horoscope for the birth of the British Princess Margaret in 1930.

In good and bad humour

For more than 2,000 years, the prevailing model of the mind and the body was rooted in the theories of Hippocrates and, later, Galen (see page 49). These early physicians accounted for the health of mind and body, and aspects of temperament or personality, through humoral theory. Four substances, called 'humours', were thought to occur in varying proportions in the human body: namely, blood, phlegm, yellow bile and black bile.

Six hundred years separate the Ancient Greek physician Hippocrates of Cos (*c.*460–370BC) from Galen of Pergamon (AD130–210), a Greek physician living in the Roman Empire.

Like Hippocrates, Galen compiled a compendium of all medical knowledge current at the time, contributing his own research and ideas. For both Hippocrates and Galen, fitness and sickness of both body and mind were controlled by the balance of the humours. When these were in their proper proportions, the body and mind were healthy. When there was an unnatural preponderance or lack of one, sickness resulted, and health returned only once the humours were in balance.

The balance of the humours would change according to diet, activity, age and lifestyle, as well as illness. In addition, each individual was said to have a different natural temperament. Some people had a naturally high level of yellow bile, for instance, and were therefore said to have a choleric temperament. These people are defined as quick to anger. A person with a higher level of blood than the other humours would be said to have a sanguine temperament. If a person had a preponderance of black bile, they would be of a melancholic nature. If phlegm was the dominant humour, the person would be of a calm disposition.

The humoral theory endured until the 19th century. It provided the first pseudo-biological explanation of character, one that favoured nature over nurture though elements of the environment such as diet or poor living conditions could also affect the balance of the humours and consequently the mood.

Humour	Temperament	Characteristics
Phlegm	Phlegmatic	Calm, unemotional
Blood	Sanguine	Cheerful
Yellow bile	Choleric	Quick-tempered
Black bile	Melancholic	Sad

HUMOURS AND ELEMENTS

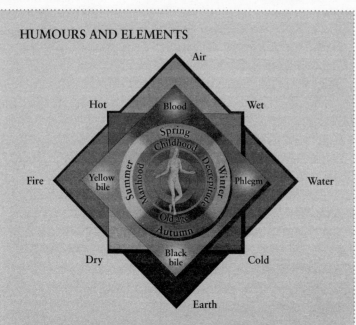

The humours were closely related to the theory of the four elements, which the Ancient Greeks believed made up all things: earth, fire, water and air. Earth was thought to correspond to black bile, fire to yellow bile, water to phlegm, and air to blood. The ages of man were linked with seasons, with youth correlating to spring and old age to winter, and a person's humoral profile would correspondingly change with their age.

Crafty science

The belief that a person's character can be read in their face has been around since Ancient Greece. The idea was common in Europe during the Middle Ages, and some universities were teaching how to tell character from facial features well into the Renaissance era. Humoral theory lent itself to a system of determining character from appearance. Because the proportion of humours affected the physical as well as the mental state of an individual, it seemed likely that there would be a correlation between appearance and temperament. An excess of any of the four humours could apparently be seen in the face (see illustration) as well as in the character. A sanguine type would have a ruddy complexion and a person with too much black bile would look sad, sallow and drawn. But Leonardo da Vinci dismissed the practice as false and without scientific foundation. All he was prepared to concede was that the lines that develop on the face with age might throw some light on character as

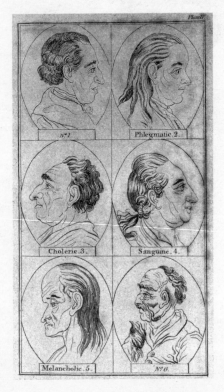

Lavater's depiction of different temperaments in physiognomy.

they could indicate types of facial expression that had become habitual, such as smiling or frowning.

In England, the Vagrancy Act of 1531 outlawed vagabonds, beggars and other travelling communities on the grounds that they were found to be

> *'using divers and subtle crafty and unlawful games and plays, and some of them feigning themselves to have knowledge in physic, physiognomy, palmistry, or other crafty sciences . . . to the great deceit of the king's subjects.'*

Physiognomy had, by this point, come to be regarded as just another tool in the trickster's canon – a 'crafty science' deployed dishonestly to cozen and cheat.

Physiognomy was revived in the 18th century by the Swiss poet and pastor Johann Kaspar Lavater (1741–1801), who believed that 'an exact relationship exists between the soul and the body', and introduced the notion that physiognomy relates to specific character traits of individuals. He promoted the idea that physical beauty denotes moral worth. Although subjected to sustained criticism and sometimes ridicule during his lifetime, Lavater's work influenced the Austrian anatomist and physiologist Franz Joseph Gall (1758–1828).

BRAINS AND BUMPS
Gall was the first person to distinguish between the brain's grey matter, which contains neurons, and the white matter, which contains ganglia responsible for connections within the brain. Gall was not only convinced that different areas ('organs') of the brain carry out different tasks (called 'localization of function'), but believed that the shape of the skull reflected the precise structure of the brain. He thought that by measuring the bumps and lumps

of the skull he could determine the size of the various 'organs' and so gain detailed insight into character. His skull-measuring came to be known as phrenology. It wasn't popular with the authorities; the Church considered it anti-religious and in 1802 the Austrian government banned his lectures. Three years later he was forced to flee the country.

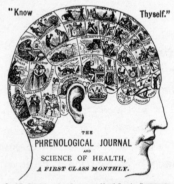

An early 19th-century phrenological map of the brain.

The German physician Johann Spurzheim (1776–1832), who worked first as Gall's assistant, developed phrenology further and popularized it in America. Influential authors such as Walt Whitman, Edgar Allan Poe, Mark Twain, Herman Melville, Emily Brontë and Charles Dickens took the subject seriously and referred to it in their books, reflecting and boosting its popular appeal.

The study of physiognomy and phrenology was carried out by Caucasian scientists who tended to discriminate along racial lines. This meant they regarded other face and head shapes as indicative of lower moral standards and meaner intelligence – more a reflection of their own depressing ignorance than that of their subjects.

DARWIN'S NOSE

The English naturalist Charles Darwin (1809–82) almost missed out on the voyage that inspired his theory of evolution because the ship's captain, Robert FitzRoy (1805–65), a keen physiognomist, very nearly rejected him for the post of ship's naturalist out of hand. He thought the shape of Darwin's nose suggested a lack of determination.

If humours and the inherited strengths and weaknesses of the brain predisposed individuals to behave in a certain way, this suggested they were strongly influenced by inherited characteristics beyond their control. In the second half of the 19th century, this powerful current of thinking reflected aspects of Darwin's theory of evolution, which was being felt throughout all aspects of science. The impact on the burgeoning field of psychology was considerable. The British psychologist Francis Galton (1822–1911), famous for his work on intelligence testing and notorious for his recommendation that the less intelligent should be discouraged from breeding, coined the term 'nature against nurture'. He came down heavily on the side of nature, supporting his case with findings from his studies of monozygotic (identical) and dizygotic (non-identical) twins.

'There are four temperaments . . . the lymphatic, the sanguine, the bilious, and the nervous. . . . The different temperaments are indicated by external signs, which are open to observation. The first, or lymphatic, is distinguishable by a round form of the body, softness of the muscular system, repletion of the cellular tissue, fair hair, and a pale skin. It is accompanied by languid vital actions, with weakness and slowness in the circulation. The brain, as part of the system, is also slow, languid, and feeble in its action, and the mental

manifestations are proportionally weak. The second or sanguine temperament, is indicated by well defined forms, moderate plumpness of person, tolerable firmness of flesh, light hair inclining to chestnut, blue eyes, and fair complexion, with ruddiness of countenance. It is marked by great activity of the blood vessels, fondness for exercise, and an animated countenance. The brain partakes of the general state, and is vigorous and active. The fibrous (generally, but inappropriately, termed the bilious) temperament is recognised by black hair, dark skin, moderate fulness and much firmness of flesh, with harshly expressed outline of the person. The functions partake of great energy of action, which extends to the brain; and the countenance, in consequence, shews strong, marked, and decided features. The nervous temperament is recognised by fine thin hair, thin skin, small thin muscles, quickness in muscular motion, paleness of countenance, and often delicate health. The whole nervous system, including the brain, is predominantly active and energetic, and the mental manifestations are proportionally vivacious and powerful.'

The English science writer and lecturer William Mattieu Williams (1820–92), in *A Vindication of Phrenology* (1894, published posthumously)

Galton and others attempted to extend Darwin's principle of natural selection to the realm of society, an approach now labelled Social Darwinism. This is generally summarized as the 'survival of the fittest' and contends that the 'better' people in society will thrive, while the 'weaker' will not (or should not). It can be manifested in a *laissez-faire* capitalist system in which the sick, weak or disabled are given no financial or social support.

It has also been used to justify imperialism, racism and eugenics, with the aim of 'improving humanity' by curtailing reproduction among those groups considered to be detrimental to the gene pool – such as the chronically sick, disabled, mentally ill, homosexuals and some racial groups.

BORN CRIMINALS

The Italian criminologist and scientific racist Cesare Lombroso (1835–1909) combined aspects of Social Darwinism, psychology and physiognomy in his theory of the criminal 'type'. He regarded criminality, at least in the case of serious or persistent felons, to be a matter of heredity, and believed criminals represented throwbacks to an early stage of human evolution. His thinking on criminality, now discredited, asserted that criminals could be identified by 'ape-like' physical characteristics such as a sloping forehead, long arms, and a projecting jaw. Unusually-sized ears and an asymmetrical face or head were also considered common characteristics of criminals. Not all distinguishing features were immediately visible: Lombroso thought that criminal types had especially acute sight, decreased capacity for feeling pain, lack of remorse or moral sense, and a propensity for cruelty, vanity, impulsiveness and vindictiveness. Lombroso's theory found little support in Europe but was highly influential in the United States, where it formed the basis of criminal physiognomy.

FICTIONAL CRIMINALS

The assumption that a person's criminal nature was reflected in their appearance is found in 19th-century fiction. Charles Dickens describes the criminal Fagin in Oliver Twist *as 'a very old shrivelled Jew, whose villanous-looking and repulsive face was obscured by a quantity of matted red* hair'. *While this description is in keeping with Lavater's assertion that physiognomy relates to specific character traits, it is overlain with an anti-Semitism that is shocking to modern readers. When Dickens introduces us to the convict Magwitch in* Great Expectations, *he doesn't refer to his personal appearance, only to his clothes and physical state. Magwitch will turn out to be benign, so fitting his physiognomy to a criminal template would be misleading:*

> 'A fearful man, all in coarse grey, with a great iron
> on his leg. A man with no hat, and with broken
> shoes, and with an old rag tied round his head.
> A man who had been soaked in water, and
> smothered in mud, and lamed by stones, and cut
> by flints, and stung by nettles, and torn by briars;
> who limped, and shivered, and glared, and growled;
> and whose teeth chattered in his head as he seized
> me by the chin.'

PALM READING

Palmistry, chiromancy or chirognomy is the belief that a person's character and future can be discerned from the pattern of lines on the palm of the hand. It has a long history, and has been practised in China, Tibet, Persia, Sumeria, Ancient Israel and Mesopotamia as well as Europe. Even Hippocrates studied patients' palms during diagnosis. Aristotle commented: 'Lines are not written into the human hand without reason. They emanate from heavenly influences and man's own individuality.'

The Church suppressed palmistry in Europe during the Middle Ages, considering it a type of pagan superstition. During the Renaissance, palmistry was included along with necromancy as one of the forbidden arts. It reappeared in Europe following the publication, in 1839, of an influential treatise on the subject by a French army officer, Captain Casimir Stanislas D'Arpentigny (b.1798), who had become interested in 'chirognomy' after a gypsy girl read his palm during a military campaign in Spain. It became increasingly popular during the second half of the 19th century.

The genetic lottery

Since the publication of Darwin's theory of evolution and the work of Gregor Mendel (1822–84), who established the mechanics of hereditary characteristics, it has become generally accepted that many of our personal attributes are inherited. It is easy to spot hereditary characteristics such as eye colour and face shape; but more difficult to pinpoint genetically inherited psychological attributes. For example, how much is, say, musicality the result of heredity and how much is it the result of being raised in a household of musical people? It's difficult to disentangle the roles of heredity and environment on the development of character and, even more controversially, on 'intelligence'.

TWIN STUDIES

One way to try to determine how much of personality is inherited is through the study of identical twins. The first twin studies were carried out by Francis Galton in the 1870s. He used questionnaires to assess psychological traits, and came down heavily on the side of nature (inherited characteristics) as the most influential. The behaviourist Edward Thorndike conducted the first experimental twin studies, using 50 pairs of twins. He tested the pairs at different ages (9–10 years and 13–14 years). His results suggested that the importance of heredity decreases with age – so twins might begin with the same genetic inheritance and the same environment, but as they develop autonomy and have separate experiences, their characters diverge. The implication that both heredity and genetics affect character has been borne out by subsequent studies.

NATURE AND NURTURE IN TWINS

Monozygotic (identical) twins that have been separated from birth and raised by different families have an identical genetic makeup, but different environmental influences. By comparing them, it's possible to theorize about which characteristics are the result of genetics and which the result of environmental factors.

PHOTOGRAPHIC EVIDENCE?

In the 19th century, the invention of photography played a significant role in the development of physiognomy. People working in asylums could (and did) photograph patients of all types and in different states of illness and health. This provided wider access to a far larger bank of examples than sketches could offer. Lombroso and Galton both used photographs to establish what they believed to be criminal and psychological 'types', and the French neurologist Jean-Martin Charcot photographed patients he had placed under hypnosis to demonstrate different stages of hysteria.

THE CASE OF INTELLIGENCE

A politically explosive idea is the suggestion that intelligence can be inherited. Following his investigations on the subject, Galton suggested that those of weak intelligence should 'find a welcome refuge' as celibates in a monastery rather than run the risk of passing on their defective genes. He carried out the first study of genius, using a method he designed called 'historiometry' to determine whether intelligence is inherited. This drew on various types of biographical records to count the number of eminent relatives an individual had and to infer from that the hereditary patterns of intelligence. Galton found that the closer he kept to a straight line of descent (parent–child), the more likely he was to find a connection between eminence and heredity. The method depends on the 'intelligent' person choosing (or having access to) a field of work that allowed eminence to shine forth. Galton's results suggested that intelligence is inherited, but shed no light on the impact of an individual's environment in realizing potential intelligence.

Intelligence testing was a growth area – and big business – in the first half of the 20th century. But psychologists began to argue about its definition: Lewis Terman defined intelligence as the ability to think abstractly; Edward Thorndike emphasized learning and the ability to give good responses to questions. Even today, psychologists and other interested professionals don't agree on a definition of intelligence. There is a consensus that it is a complex synthesis of different elements, including learning, reasoning, problem-solving and creativity and is not about excelling in a single intellectual activity.

CATCHING ON
'A very general mental capability that, among other things, involves the ability to reason, plan, solve problems, think

abstractly, comprehend complex ideas, learn quickly and learn from experience. It is not merely book learning, a narrow academic skill, or test-taking smarts. Rather, it reflects a broader and deeper capability for comprehending our surroundings – "catching on," "making sense" of things, or "figuring out" what to do.'

American educational psychologist
Linda S. Gottfredson (b.1947)

TESTING INTELLIGENCE

Francis Galton was the first psychologist to test intelligence. He favoured the nature-over-nurture model and in 1865 suggested giving evolution a helping hand through selective breeding, which he named 'eugenics'.

The French psychologists Alfred Binet and Theodore Simon developed the first widely used, intellect-based testing for children in 1905. The Binet–Simon scale of intelligence rated their subjects against the normal level of skills for their age. In 1911, William Stern divided intellectual age as revealed by the Binet–Simon tests by chronological age. In 1916, Lewis Terman multiplied Stern's figures by 100 to give the now-familiar IQ (intelligence quotient) scale:

$$IQ = \frac{Intellectual\ age}{Chronological\ age} \times 100$$

Binet later expressed dismay regarding the simplistic way in which his and Simon's test had been applied.

What makes you 'you'?

Locke, who believed in the *tabula rasa* model, regarded education as of paramount importance:

> '*I think I may say that of all the men we meet with, nine parts of ten are what they are, good or evil, useful or not, by their education.*'

He warned that we should be especially careful about the type of ideas and stimuli to which young children are exposed, because the first marks made on them are very important:

> '*The little and almost insensible impressions on our tender infancies have very important and lasting consequences.*'

Like Locke, Jean-Jacques Rousseau believed in the *tabula rasa* concept. He thought human nature was essentially noble and good, but corrupted by society. As a child, every individual was, in his view, innately noble and virtuous and had immense potential – potential which was sadly almost always wasted. With this idea of the 'noble savage', Rousseau saw civilization making uncorrupted man a slave to unnatural desires and generally laying waste to his potential:

> '*Everything is good as it leaves the hands of the Author of things; everything degenerates in the hands of man.*'

His most famous pronouncement – '*Man is born free, but is everywhere in chains*' – underlines this philosophy.

David Hume, a contemporary of Rousseau, took a middle path, not supposing humans to be either innately noble or innately selfish. What we encounter in life, coupled with our individual mix of passions, determines what we learn and how we will respond to future events. Starting from neither a propensity to good (savage nobility) nor ill (rampant selfishness), the individual is moulded by his or her experiences and the ways that they respond to them. Hume believed that accumulated experiences and responses make our lives, and every idea we have originates from a sense-impression we once experienced.

But Hume was wary of saying there is a definable 'self' at the centre of the 'bundle of perceptions'; different experiences would have produced a different person, and you would not be the same person if you had had a different upbringing, or lived in a very different environment.

'Some recent philosophers seem to have given their moral approval to these deplorable verdicts that affirm that the intelligence of an individual is a fixed quantity, a quantity that cannot be augmented. We must protest and react against this brutal pessimism; we will try to demonstrate that it is founded on nothing.'

Alfred Binet, *Les idées modernes sur les enfants* (1909)

THE 'SELF'

The notion of 'self' exploded on to the scene with the work of Sigmund Freud in the 1890s. His account of the psyche had two aspects that were innate (the id and the ego) and one aspect, the superego, which had been built up during childhood from internalized ideals acquired from parental and societal influences. In brief, the id represents instincts, the superego represents morality and the ego takes a realistic position trying to negotiate between them. The values of the superego are culturally determined, so the impact of environment and experience is paramount. According to Freud, we all share basic instinctual drives, which are represented by the id. How far we follow these drives is determined by the interaction of the superego's drive towards morality and the compromises made by the ego. To illustrate his theory, Freud compared the id to a horse, while the ego is 'like a man on horseback, who has to hold in check the superior strength of the horse'. Comprising both the conscience and the ideal self, the superego produces a drive towards perfection. Conflict between the three aspects of the psyche results in psychological discomfort and, if not addressed, mental illness. Invariably, Freud found the sex drive to be at the root of most problems with character.

For Freud, the unconscious controlled the mind. Because, by its very nature, we can't examine the unconscious directly, we need to look for other ways to access it. One way was through dreams, and another through the free association practised in psychoanalysis. Freud's model is highly deterministic, with early experiences causing certain predictable outcomes in terms of character (and neurosis) in adulthood.

CHILD PRODIGIES

In a series of studies in the early 21st century, L. R. Vandervert used a brain imaging technique called positron emission tomography (PET) scanning to examine the brain activity of child prodigies. He found that some parts of the brain of gifted people (those areas relevant to their particular skill) are better developed than in the less gifted. In particular, they made more use of long-term memory.

Chess teacher László Polgár set out to raise his three daughters as world-class chess players and succeeded, although as he clearly had a talent for chess, heredity cannot be ruled out as a factor. The German composer George Frideric Handel had innate musical talent that thrived despite his home environment. Although he was not encouraged by his parents, he emerged as a musical genius:

'He had discovered such a strong propensity to Music, that his father who always intended him for the study of the Civil Law, had reason to be alarmed. He strictly forbade him to meddle with any musical instrument but Handel found means to get a little clavichord privately convey'd to a room at the top of the house. To this room he constantly stole when the family was asleep.'

Handel's first biographer, John Mainwaring (1760)

CIRCLES OF EGO AND SELF

Carl Jung, originally an enthusiastic supporter of Freud, criticized his emphasis on infant sexuality and focus on sexual energy as the main driving force in human behaviour. He thought the ego represented the conscious mind – its thoughts, memories and emotions and a person's own sense of their identity. Like Freud,

A representation of the 'self' in Jungian psychology, with the ego as a smaller circle inside it.

he also believed in the importance of the unconscious, but he divided it into two parts, the personal and the collective unconscious. Jung maintained that the self includes all aspects of personality, including the conscious and unconscious minds and the ego.

According to Jung, the ultimate aim of every person is to achieve a state of selfhood. From birth, every individual has a sense of the self, but a separate ego-consciousness grows out of this in the first half of life. Once the person is securely rooted in the external world, there is a return to and a conscious rediscovery of the self in the second half of life. Coming to terms with our own personality is often prompted by some kind of psychic wounding brought about by events (external factors). Jung's psychology often has a spiritual or mystical flavour, and this redefining of the self in the second half of life involves integration with or recognition of archetypes:

'The Self . . . embraces ego-consciousness, shadow, anima, and collective unconscious in indeterminable extension. As a totality, the self is a coincidentia oppositorum; it is therefore bright and dark and yet neither.'

'The Self is the total, timeless man . . . who stands for the mutual integration of conscious and unconscious.'

The goal of totality and of the consolidation and acceptance of the self would be recalled in Abraham Maslow's humanistic psychology and his focus on self-actualization (see pages 193–4 and 216–17).

The Austrian psychiatrist Alfred Adler was one of the first of the Vienna Psychoanalytic Society to break away from Freud. He believed that the self should be considered a unified whole, and he rejected the split into id, ego and superego as unhelpful. For Adler, the individual was connected to a surrounding world and external events and influences were as important as the internal struggles that Freud put at the heart of his model of psychic development. Adler considered other powerful dynamics, including gender and politics, to be just as important as libido. Freud disagreed with Adler's 'individual psychology' and described his views as 'honourable errors'.

Adler emphasized the important part that feelings of inferiority play in personality development. This 'inferiority complex' is thought to drive afflicted individuals to overcompensate, resulting either in extraordinary achievement and success or extremely asocial behaviour.

In keeping with his belief that the relationship between a child and the surrounding family and wider society creates the child's feelings of power or impotence, Adler advocated training children to be and feel an equal part of the family, to learn how to make decisions and cooperate. He recommended that not only parents, but also teachers, nurses, social workers and so on, be trained in parent education so that children develop a healthy level of self-esteem. Adler taught that this prevents feelings of superiority or inferiority and the associated compensatory behaviours which cause problems in later life.

Adler promoted the view that analyst and patient are equal partners in a conversation; he also advocated the need for female analysts. He believed that birth order had an influence upon a person's psychological makeup. For example, he observed that firstborn children were in a favourable position because they received the full attention of their parents. But they suffered feelings of 'dethronement' when younger siblings came along and usurped their position. He said that youngest children were likely to be overindulged, resulting in poor social empathy. Therefore, the middle child or children were likely to be the most balanced, as they had experienced neither of these fates. Adler's speculations were not based in scientific evidence. But he was satisfied that they answered the question: 'Why do children who are raised in the same family grow up with very different personalities?'

Although he believed the individual's experiences as a child would mould their later life as an adult, Adler also stressed that we are free to create what we will from the experiences we have gained, although it requires conscious effort. Even bad experiences can be put to constructive use by the 'creative self':

> 'We do not suffer the shock of [traumas], we make out of them what suits our purposes.'

We make our own beliefs and then live as if they are true, hence forging our own identities and lives, even in the face of adversity.

All around you

For the behaviourists, who didn't believe in inherited mental content, the impact of the familial environment on behaviour was all there was. As John B. Watson put it:

> 'All of the weaknesses, reserves, fears, cautions, and inferiorities of our parents are stamped into us with sledge-hammer blows.'

With this degree of power in the hands of parents, the developmental psychologists felt they had a huge responsibility to explain how best to wield it.

STYLE OF LIFE

Adler saw childhood experiences manifest themselves later in the individual's 'style of life' – the unique, unconscious and repetitive way in which he or she approaches the main tasks of living: friendship, work and love. If there were problems, Adler believed they could only be altered by in-depth psychoanalysis. He identified four main styles of life, the first three of which he described as 'mistaken styles':

- *Ruling type: this describes aggressive, dominating people who don't have much social interest or cultural perception.*
- *Getting type: dependent people who take rather than give.*
- *Avoiding type: people who try to escape life's problems and take little part in socially constructive activity.*
- *Socially useful type: people who take great interest in others and engage in a lot of social activity.*

STAMPING OUT INDIVIDUALITY

The American psychologist and educator Granville Stanley Hall (1844–1924) was an influential pioneer in educational psychology. His aim was not to develop the individual potential of a child, but to mould him or her into a useful member of society. Hall considered the cult of the individual to be iniquitous and misguided, and thought it threatened to destroy America. His attitude towards childrearing was akin to beast-taming.

Hall was influenced by Darwin's theory of evolution by natural selection and by the theory of 'recapitulation' proposed by German biologist and philosopher Ernst Haeckel (1834–1919), which states that in its embryonic stages an organism recalls all the stages of the organism's evolutionary development. (For example, the human embryo at one point resembles a fish, so we can deduce that humans had a fish-like ancestor.) Hall believed that in growing from babyhood to adulthood, we replay the psychologies of different stages of human evolution, starting as savages.

Hall believed that as a child reaches adolescence, a note of altruism replaces their inherent selfishness so it becomes appropriate to inculcate patriotism, military obedience, love of authority, awe at nature and selfless devotion to God and state. He didn't see any point in schools striving towards intellectual attainment, as the last thing he wanted to see in American youth was any individuality that might lead to independent thought or the questioning of authority. He referred to the 'storm and stress' of adolescence, and advised that the sexes be separately educated, to avoid distraction and ensure that boys and girls could be guided towards their natural roles. He strongly disapproved of only children, saying that, 'being an only child is a disease in itself'. In 1896 he supervised a study of only children which found them largely to be maladjusted misfits.

Hall helped to originate the study of developmental psychology from infancy to old age (he wrote an influential text on the psychology of ageing) but also, by bringing Darwinism into psychology, in establishing the functionalist school.

'If there be an order in which the human race has mastered its various kinds of knowledge, there will arise in every child an aptitude to acquire these kinds of knowledge in the same order. . . . Education is a repetition of civilization in little.'

English sociologist and philosopher
Herbert Spencer (1861)

SEEN AND NOT HEARD

In the late 19th and early 20th centuries, the general attitude towards children was that they should be strictly disciplined, never indulged and largely just endured until they could grow into useful citizens. The views of the behaviourist psychologist John B. Watson were both typical and influential. His advice on childcare was still being heeded in the 1950s:

> *'Never hug and kiss them, never let them sit in your lap. If you must, kiss them once on the forehead when they say goodnight. Shake hands with them in the morning. . . . When you are tempted to pet your child remember that mother love is a dangerous instrument. An instrument which may inflict a never-healing wound, a wound which may make infancy unhappy, adolescence a nightmare, an instrument which may wreck your adult son or daughter's vocational future and their chances for marital happiness.'*

Watson was confident that we can make anything we want out of people – parental discipline can control the destiny of children, and psychologists can become social engineers.

Defending parental love

It was against the background of Hall's and Watson's attitudes to parenting, and the prevailing view that the maternal bond with the child hinges on nutrition, that the British psychologist and psychoanalyst John Bowlby (1907–90) and the American psychiatrist Harry Harlow carried out their work on the mother–child relationship.

Bowlby was particularly interested in the way family relationships could lead to either well-adjusted or maladjusted children and adults. He found that secure attachment, manifested in a strong bond between primary carer (generally the mother) and infant, is essential to the psychological well-being of a child. This was the exact opposite of Watson's view. Bowlby was influenced by Lorenz's work on imprinting and drew on it to explore instinctive behaviour in babies. He concluded that the infant has an instinctive drive to form a close primary bond with one attachment figure (though more bonds are possible). The child has innate behaviours, such as crying and smiling, that encourage the caregiver to interact and stay close to the child. The behaviour of the caregiver is also innate. Failure to form such a bond can lead to psychological and physiological problems including aggression, failure to flourish, reduced intelligence, depression, and even 'affectionless psychopathy' (characterized by an inability to show care, concern or affection for others, and a tendency to show little remorse, guilt or shame for their bad deeds).

Through laboratory experiments, Bowlby found that if a child is separated from the primary attachment figure for a short period, he or she will become distressed. If the separation continues, the child will appear seemingly calmer, but actually become withdrawn and uninterested in anything. If it continues even longer the child will begin to interact with others, but will reject the caregiver and show anger on their return. Bowlby listed the stages as protest, despair and depression. His advice, in 1951, was that the child should have continuous care from the primary attachment figure for the first two years of life, and should not be needlessly separated from them for the first five years. If a child fails to form a secure attachment in the first year or two, the window of opportunity closes and irreparable psychological and emotional damage is done. The idea of a critical period accords with Lorenz's findings with his goslings. The optimum period for imprinting was, Lorenz found, 12–17 hours after hatching; if the goslings were not allowed to imprint within 32 hours it was too late and it would not happen at all.

A TWO-YEAR-OLD GOES TO HOSPITAL

In 1952, Bowlby and his colleague, the Scottish psychoanalyst James Robertson (1911–88), made a short

> film that showed the distress a small child experiences in
> hospital when temporarily separated from his parents. The
> film changed the way hospitals treated young patients, in
> particular changing the visiting hours to allow parents
> much more contact with their children. Bowlby's work with
> the World Health Organization guided the treatment of
> orphaned children in the aftermath of World War II.

Bowlby's findings clearly raise contentious issues, including the possibility that putting an infant into full-time, long-term day-care might have deleterious effects on the child. Predictably, they attracted criticism. It was argued that he did not distinguish between children who failed to form an attachment in the first place and those who formed an attachment that was then broken – through illness or the death of the parent, for example. It was also said that he ascribed insufficient value to other strong bonds, such as with a second parent, grandparents or siblings.

In 1981, the child psychiatrist Michael Rutter (b.1933) distinguished between the failure to form an emotional bond (privation) and the breaking of a bond that has already formed (deprivation), regarding the former to be the more harmful.

Bowlby remained convinced that attachment formed the bedrock of the process by which the child learns how to be a person. The child, he says, learns how to interact with others from the caregiver, and bases the model of their own identity on the way in which the caregiver responds to them. His findings are largely supported by later research. Harry Harlow's brutal experiments on deprivation in infant monkeys and several studies involving children kept in institutions support the view that lack of attachment leads to emotional disturbance, physical and psychological ill-health and delayed or arrested development.

44 THIEVES

Bowlby studied a group of 44 young people labelled as delinquents who were attending a clinic after being found guilty of crimes. He compared them with a control group of 44 young people with non-crime-related issues. He discovered that, compared with the control group, a higher proportion of the delinquents had endured periods of separation from their mothers in early childhood and showed signs of affectionless psychopathy. He concluded that maternal deprivation led to their problems of delinquency and psychopathy. Later commentators have pointed out that although his results show correlation, causation can't be inferred. Other factors, such as diet and poverty, could also have contributed to their behaviour.

In 1989, developmental psychologists Jill Hodges and Barbara Tizard carried out research into a group of children who had spent their early years in institutions. They found that those who were adopted by the age of four had been able to form strong attachments with their new families and did not develop affectionless psychopathy. This later study suggests the effects need not be as dire and irreversible as Bowlby suggested, at least as long as a child is given a chance of stable affection during their early years.

DEPRIVATION AND DEPRESSION

The American psychologist Harry Harlow (1905–81) also explored the importance to an infant of attachment to the mother. In 1958, he was raising monkeys to use as experimental animals when he noticed that those hand-reared in isolation were psychologically different from monkeys kept with their mothers.

To investigate the role of the mother, he carried out a series of (unethical) experiments that involved separating baby monkeys from their mothers and rearing some of them in isolation for up to 24 months. The isolated monkeys grew up to be intensely mentally disturbed.

Harlow made surrogate monkey mothers from wire and wood, some of which he covered with cloth. He put a cloth mother and a wire mother in each baby monkey's cage. One of the two was fitted with a feeding bottle. The baby monkeys all preferred the cloth mothers, whether or not they held the feeding bottle. If the wire mother had the bottle, the baby would go to it only to feed and then return to the cloth-covered mother for comfort. Each baby monkey had its own surrogate mother, and grew attached to it, learning to recognize it and preferring it to other similar ones. Baby monkeys placed in a new environment with their cloth mothers would explore their surroundings, returning

frequently to the mother for comfort. Baby monkeys left alone in the new environment did not explore, but showed behaviour associated with extreme distress (such as curling up and screaming).

Harlow concluded that nourishment is not the most important aspect of the mother–child bond.

Harry Harlow presents a baby monkey with a wireframe 'mother'.

PIT OF DESPAIR

Harry Harlow carried out experiments in which he kept monkeys in darkness and isolation in a tank he provocatively called the 'pit of despair'. The monkeys quickly became disturbed and depressed. He then examined their depressive state and tried to heal it:

'In our study of psychopathology, we began as sadists trying to produce abnormality. Today we are psychiatrists trying to achieve normality and equanimity.'

Harlow's experiments were often considered unethical even at the time and it has been suggested that they prompted the animal liberation movement in the USA.

In 1946, the American paediatrician Benjamin Spock (1903–98) published *The Common Sense Book of Baby and Child Care*. In it, he denounced the practices promoted by the behaviourists who advocated training babies by leaving them to cry, enforcing strict feeding times and sleep routines, and withholding affection. Spock recommended that parents follow their instincts, give affection and vary their practice to suit the character of the individual child.

The book was a bestseller and became highly influential. Later, critics of the perceived social problems of the second half of the 20th century (such as sexual liberation) put the blame squarely on Spock and his 'permissive' approach to childrearing. Conservative detractors claimed that by encouraging indulgence, he had contributed to a generation of people with an exaggerated sense of entitlement and no moral fibre, though Spock's supporters argued that these criticisms betrayed an ignorance of what he had actually written.

> 'The surest way to raise mentally healthy children is to cultivate loving, nurturing, and mutually respectful relationships with them. Loving means, first of all, accepting your child as a person. Every child has strengths and weaknesses, gifts and challenges. Loving means adjusting your expectations to fit your child, not trying to adjust your child to fit your expectations.'
>
> Benjamin Spock, *The Common Sense Book of Baby and Child Care* (1946)

THE ROMANIAN ORPHANAGES

Under the rule of Nicolae Ceauşescu in Romania, up to 170,000 children were kept in orphanages in abject squalor. They were subject to abuse and neglect, often kept tied to their cots, lying in their own filth, undernourished and never washed, picked up or shown affection. In 1989, a number of charities moved in to help the orphans. Psychologists were able to study the children over many years while attempts were made to rehabilitate them.

Many of the children suffered lasting physical and psychological effects. This included impaired intelligence and stunted growth. They had failed to produce growth hormones, and the lack of intellectual and emotional stimulation had prevented normal development. Some of those rescued from the orphanages at a young age and placed with loving foster families made a good recovery, but for many, and especially those who had spent longer in the institutions, the damage was irreversible.

Becoming yourself

The humanistic psychologists of the late 20th century focused on the conscious, chosen development and perfection of the self. For them, whatever upbringing we have had, we all have the potential to be in control of forging our later selves. The ultimate goal for the human was, in Abraham Maslow's term, self-actualization.

German-American psychologist Kurt Lewin (1890–1947) pursued the idea that behaviour results from the interaction of the individual and their environment. Initially a behaviourist, Lewin discovered an interest in Gestalt psychology while volunteering in the German army during World War I. He believed that people had thoughts, forces and emotions which altered their behaviour to reflect their current state. Lewin coined the term 'life space' to describe this combination of factors.

According to Lewin, behaviour could be expressed as a function of life space. He expressed this simple idea in pseudo-scientific notation as the formula:

$B = f(LS)$ where B is Behaviour and LS is Life Space

Lewin believed that needs produced tensions which the individual would try to resolve. Needs could be biological (such as thirst) or psychological (such as wanting a to be wealthy). A need would dominate the life space to a greater or lesser degree until it was resolved. Lewin delineated different types of conflict within individuals, which he summarized as:

- Approach–approach conflict: experienced by a person wanting two attractive options and having to choose just one (such as two holiday destinations).

- Avoidance–avoidance conflict: experienced by a person having to choose between two disagreeable options (such as an unpleasant surgical procedure or long-term discomfort).

- Approach–avoidance conflict: experienced by a person with a single goal which has potentially both positive and negative characteristics (such as starting up a new business) and which involves risk and hard work, but offers excitement, independence and the opportunity for financial success.

COGNITIVE DISSONANCE

One of those most influenced by Lewin was the American psychologist Leon Festinger (1919–89), who in 1957 devised the theory of 'cognitive dissonance'. His two basic hypotheses were as follows:

- Psychological discomfort (dissonance) will motivate an individual to try to reduce the dissonance and achieve consonance.

- While trying to reduce the dissonance, an individual will actively avoid situations and information that are likely to increase it.

Cognitive dissonance arises when our behaviour conflicts with beliefs that are integral to our idea of ourselves. Say, for example, you think of yourself as a healthy and fit person, but spend the weekend slobbing out eating doughnuts on the sofa. You may tell yourself that this is a 'reward' for your stint in the gym. Or you might minimize the risks of eating doughnuts by telling yourself that they are not unhealthy really. You might tell yourself that if you become hooked on fitness you will become boring and your friends won't like you. By using such explanations, you reduce the dissonance and continue the pattern of behaviour.

Festinger and fellow psychologist James Merrill Carlsmith (1936–84) employed a group of students to carry out a dull task. The participants were then paid either $1 or $20 to tell the next group of students that the task was interesting. When later questioned about the task, those who were paid $20 said it was boring, but those who were paid only $1 rated it as more interesting. The researchers explained this result in terms of cognitive dissonance. The students who received $20 felt they had been paid well enough, so did not need to pretend to themselves that the task was interesting. But the students who received $1 either had to admit to themselves that they had lied for a small reward, or they had to change their view of the task. It was easier to admit they had been wrong in their opinion of the task than to accept that they had lied in exchange for a tiny reward.

> 'Dissonance theory does not rest upon the assumption that man is a rational animal; rather, it suggests that man is a rationalizing animal – that he attempts to appear rational, both to others and to himself.'
> **Elliot Aronson, *Theories of Cognitive Consistency* (1968)**

Carlsmith undertook another study in cognitive dissonance by testing a group of children in 1963 with fellow US psychologist Elliot Aronson (b.1932). A child was left alone in a room with lots of toys and was told they could play with all of them but one, which was extra special. Half of the children in the group were threatened with a serious punishment if they played with the special toy. The other half were threatened with a mild punishment. None of the children disobeyed. Later, the children were allowed to play with any toy, including the special one. Those threatened with a mild punishment were less likely to play with the prohibited toy than the other children. Carlsmith and Aronson suggested that the children rationalized their response to the mild threat by persuading themselves that the toy was not really interesting, so they didn't want to play with it.

This recalls Piaget's account of how children adjust their schemata to accommodate new experiences or information. In the case of cognitive dissonance, it is the person's schema for him- or herself that is threatened by the mismatch between act and belief, so the schema is adjusted to accommodate the behaviour.

> 'If a person is induced to do or say something which is contrary to his private opinion, there will be a tendency for him to change his opinion so as to bring it into correspondence with what he has done or said.'
>
> **Leon Festinger and J. Merrill Carlsmith**

HOW WE PERCEIVE OURSELVES

In 1972, the American social psychologist Daryl J. Bem (b.1938) proposed an alternative to cognitive dissonance; he called it 'self-perception theory'. This held that people infer their attitudes from their own behaviour rather than the other way round. Our usual assumption works like this: if you think of yourself as interested in cycling, you may buy a good-quality bike and go for long rides. But Bem viewed it the other way round. He said you could infer that you are interested in cycling because you have bought an expensive bike and used it many times; in this way, behaviour shapes attitude.

Subsequent studies have shown that attitudes and emotions at least do follow behaviours. In 1974, the American psychologist

James Laird demonstrated how changes in facial expression can trigger changes in emotion. By asking test participants to smile or frown, he recorded their reactions and discovered that they reported feeling angrier when frowning and happier when smiling. Laird spent his career studying aspects of self-perception theory and remained convinced that feelings are the consequence, not the cause, of behaviour.

BECOMING A WHOLE PERSON

More than 2,000 years ago, Aristotle considered that the aim of life was to become a whole person, living according to one's moral standards and values, and that this was the source of happiness. One could be happy, in Aristotle's terms, even in prison and when persecuted as long as one's integrity was intact. It's a view that has never been out of fashion for long with philosophers, but was only explored thoroughly by psychology in the 20th century, with the work of Carl Jung and the humanistic psychologists Abraham Maslow and Carl Rogers (1902–87). Jung, as we have seen, saw the goal of the second half of life as consolidation and acceptance of the self, becoming a 'total [hu]man'.

Maslow put self-actualization at the pinnacle of his 'pyramid of needs' (see pages 216–17). This five-tier model describes the needs Maslow believed drove all human activity. He prioritized them, starting with physiological needs (for example, for food) and then the need for safety. When basic needs are met, or nearly met, the individual can attend to the highest tier of the pyramid, 'growth needs', or self-actualization.

Maslow recognised that the self-actualization would take different forms for different people, but made the generalisation that the self-actualized person would be:

- Happy to embrace the unknown and the ambiguous;

- Accepting of themselves, with all their flaws;
- Motivated by growth rather than the satisfaction of needs;
- Having purpose, or a mission;
- Not troubled by small things;
- Grateful;
- Humble;
- Capable of consistently making their own decisions.

The following people can be considered to personify self-actualization: Mahatma Gandhi, Nelson Mandela, Albert Einstein, William James, Sigmund Freud, Eleanor Roosevelt and Abraham Lincoln. While the safety needs of several of them may have been threatened (both Gandhi and Mandela risked their lives for the purposes of freedom), they managed to rise through Maslow's 'hierarchy' of needs, motivated by strong conviction. Prioritizing other values above their 'safety needs' made their lives meaningful and exemplary.

Carl Rogers considered childhood experience to be the main factor in determining whether someone will become self-actualized, and that many will not. Maslow agreed that most people, perhaps 98 per cent, will never achieve self-actualization.

> 'The organism has one basic tendency and striving – to actualize, maintain, and enhance the experiencing organism.'
>
> Carl Rogers (1951)

End of the self?
Some social and cognitive psychologists in the late 20th and early 21st century have queried the validity of the concept of the self as

a 'thing' at the heart of cognition. Instead the 'self' is something that emerges from overlapping cognitive processes. Self-categorization theory, developed by the British psychologist John Turner (1947–2011), suggests that we define ourselves in terms of our membership of groups, from family to the human race as a whole. In belonging to a group, we consider the similarities we share with its members, and the differences between us and members of other groups. We use identification with groups to depersonalize ourselves in some ways, according to Turner. So, if a man identifies himself as part of an army, he will stress the ways in which he is the same as other soldiers. Externally, this is shown by conforming to the requirements or expectations of the group – wearing a uniform, obeying orders and so on. Self-categorization can change with time and circumstances.

Our membership of groups is at its widest in our membership of the human race. For all the psychological characteristics and processes that mark us out as individuals, there is a lot we share with other humans – and not all of it is pleasant or comfortable.

The Self and Society

'[The] whole spiritual heritage of mankind's evolution [is] born anew in the brain structure of every individual.'
Carl Jung (1875–1961)

While personal experiences do much to build our individual minds, there is also a good deal that is common to all people. The human condition is what unites us. Psychology is as much concerned with what connects us as the differences between us.

Nurture suppressing nature

Two philosophers who shared the view that living as part of society suppresses our basic urges and behaviour had totally opposite views of what that 'natural' human state was like. The English philosopher Thomas Hobbes (1588–1679) believed that in their natural, 'uncivilized' state humans would be driven solely by selfishness and would quickly resort to violence – life would be 'nasty, brutish and short'. However, Jean-Jacques Rousseau, writing a hundred years later, thought that natural man had an innate dignity and nobility. Neither philosopher, though, had any empirical evidence in support of the 'natural' human state he was proposing.

Our mental toolkit

Darwin influenced the development of functionalism and behaviourism by setting out that a successful organism is one that survives and reproduces. Human behaviour, like that of animals, can be investigated and explained in terms of how well any type of behaviour serves the ends of survival and reproduction. This is the subject matter of evolutionary psychology.

If the brain has evolved to be fit for purpose, to fulfil certain functions to aid the survival of both the individual and the human species, it seems to do so by equipping each child with a starter-pack of useful instincts, mental structures, processes and behaviours.

COMMON STRUCTURES

The structuralists and functionalists both worked from the assumption that it was possible to discover aspects of the mind that were common to all people. These would pattern thought and perception, and ensure a certain degree of conformity. Darwinian evolution gave a particular impetus to functionalism, as the functions of the mind must surely be those that would make it most fit for purpose, for ensuring the survival of the individual and their reproductive success?

Recent research into disgust and fear suggests there is a strong and apparently innate disgust response to many things that herald or signify disease, including vomit, faeces, rats and cockroaches, and to animals that recall mucus or pus, such as slugs and leeches. Whether these are the result of common mental structures and functions or part of a collective 'genetic memory' (like Jung's collective unconscious) is unclear. Genetic memory is generally disregarded by current psychologists.

We have already considered some of the ways in which the brain or mind has been thought to demonstrate common features, shared by us all. There are Jung's archetypes and collective unconscious, the propensity to build schemata and the possible special structuring of the brain/mind to make it receptive to language-learning.

LAMARCKIAN INHERITANCE AND BAD SMELLS

Lamarck's theory of evolution through the inheritance of acquired characteristics (see page 123) was replaced by Darwin's theory of evolution by natural selection and has been largely ignored and even ridiculed for the last 150 years. But Lamarck might yet have the last laugh. Modern research into epigenetics suggests that some adaptations to the environment may indeed be passed on to the next generation. This is thought to work through changes in the epigenome, the control mechanism that regulates gene expression by turning genes on or off.

Research published in 2013 by American behavioural psychologists Brian Dias and Kerry Ressler found that when mice were conditioned to fear a smell, their offspring also responded with sensitivity and negative responses to the same smell, even though they had not themselves been conditioned

> *to dislike it. The offspring had been produced using in vitro fertilization; they had not had contact with their biological parents, so could not have learned the fear from them.*

THE COMMON CHILDHOOD

Although Freud's method of psychoanalysis is very much concerned with personal histories and their outcomes, he drew conclusions from his cases that he applied to the human race in general. His description of the ego, superego and the id (see pages 33–4) proposes a common structure to all minds. Further, his account of how we all develop through the oral, anal and genital stages, how all children are affected by an Oedipus complex (see page 231) and how every type of neurosis can be traced back to some type of sexual exploitation or event (real or imagined) suggests a greater degree of commonality.

It's worth remembering, though, that Freud based his conclusions about all human nature on his own recollections of childhood and what he could discover from his patients through hypnosis, free association and extensive discussion. It is a big leap to assume that the experiences of the middle classes in 19th-century Vienna can be extended to people living in very different circumstances, times and places.

Are we good or bad?

Hobbes thought natural humans would fight each other in an orgy of selfishness; Rousseau believed humans displayed nobility and dignity in their natural state. Who was right?

THE LEGACY OF THE NAZIS

The Holocaust was one of the most horrific crimes of the 20th century and, indeed, of all human history. In its aftermath, people around the world asked what could drive one human being to treat another the way that SS concentration camp guards had treated their victims? What had happened to ordinary German people to make them capable of such atrocities? The question was especially pertinent to social psychologists, and several famous experiments in the years after the Second World War sought to explore the state of mind that could lead to cruelty on such a mass scale. This was not an event that could be laid entirely at the feet of a few deranged individuals; it required an explanation that took account of the enormous number of perpetrators and their previously good character – their roles as ordinary workers, fathers, husbands and friends.

FREE REIGN TO COMMIT HARM

In 1971, the American psychologist Philip Zimbardo (b.1933) set up an experiment in Stanford University to explore the interaction between prison staff and their prisoners. He recruited healthy male volunteers who were allocated roles as either prisoner or guard.

Around 1939, in Czechoslovakia, crowds line the streets to greet a parade of Nazi troops.

The experience was made as realistic as possible for the prisoners, beginning with arrest at an antisocial hour and in full view of their neighbours. The prisoners were given dehumanizing uniforms and addressed only by number. The guards were also given a uniform, including dark glasses. The guards were allowed to use any methods they wished in order to keep the prisoners under control.

The 'prison' was an adapted corridor in the psychology department of Stanford University. The doors had steel bars, the 'exercise yard' was a corridor, and there was a converted cupboard for use as a cell for solitary confinement. Prisoners slept three to a bare cell with just enough space for their beds.

As the guards began to assert their authority, prisoners were frequently woken at night to be counted. The guards were allowed to punish prisoners and often did so by forcing them to do push-ups. Nazi concentration camp guards had done the same, and US soldiers later did so in the US military prison Abu Ghraib, in Iraq. One of Zimbardo's guards stepped on the prisoners' backs or made other prisoners do so during these push-ups.

The second day, the prisoners rebelled. The guards used fire extinguishers to drive them back, then stripped the prisoners naked and put the ringleader into solitary confinement. Soon the guards moved on to methods of psychological control. They singled out some prisoners for special treatment, then arbitrarily switched their favours, so causing disorientation, dissent and distrust within the group. A day and a half into the experiment, the first of the prisoners started to suffer mental breakdown. Yet even the experimenters were now so deeply immersed in the prison mentality that they accused him of faking his distress. It was several days before he was removed from the experiment. When the experimenters heard of a planned escape, instead of observing the behaviour they became focused on preventing the break-out. To punish the prisoners, the guards forced them to clean toilets with their toothbrushes.

The study had been scheduled to last 14 days. Zimbardo called a halt to it after six, but only when visiting social psychologist Christina Maslach expressed her horror at how the prisoners were being treated. She was the only one of 50 visitors to have voiced concerns (Zimbardo married her the following year). Four of the nine prisoners had already broken down.

Zimbardo discovered three types of guard in the study. One type was tough, but treated the prisoners fairly as long as they were obedient. Another type was benevolent, doing small favours for prisoners and never punishing them. And a third type seemed to relish the power they had, finding ever more imaginative ways to hurt prisoners and abusing them when they thought they were not being observed (there were hidden cameras). There was nothing in the guards' mental profiles at the start of the experiment that Zimbardo could regard as predictive of their subsequent behaviour.

'Any deed that any human being has ever committed, however horrible, is possible for any of us – under the right circumstances. That knowledge does not excuse evil; it democratizes it, sharing its blame among ordinary actors rather than declaring it the province of deviants and despots – of Them but not Us. The primary lesson of the Stanford Prison Experiment is that situations can lead us to behave in ways we would not, could not, predict possible in advance.'

Philip Zimbardo

A FORESHADOWING OF ABU GHRAIB

Zimbardo has noted the similarities between his experiment and the prisoner abuse in the US military prison Abu Ghraib. Stripping prisoners, forcing them to stand with their head covered, and making them fake humiliating sexual acts were tactics used in Stanford and Abu Ghraib. The abuse in Abu Ghraib was blamed on 'a few bad apples', but Zimbardo has argued that there are not bad apples that spoil the barrel, but rather bad barrels that spoil the apples. The situations we put people in can either make – or allow – them to do bad things.

Zimbardo's experiment seemed to uncover a dark aspect of human nature; a willingness or even an eagerness to harm others for no good reason just because they could. He felt that anonymity aided the descent into cruelty, and the position of authority that the guards were given enabled it to happen. He noted that people quickly slipped into the roles assigned to them, so it's not possible to say whether the 'evil' guards acted out of innate evil that is usually suppressed or whether they were, at least in part, acting in the way they thought fitting for their role. Unlike the Nazi prison guards, though, no one had told them to be cruel. Where did it come from? Zimbardo has said that in these situations, past and present disappear and only the gratification of the moment counts. People do things without considering the consequences or the reasons. And no one can say that he or she would not do it. That is why it's so frightening.

> 'If only there were evil people somewhere insidiously committing evil deeds, and it were necessary only to separate them from the rest of us and destroy them. But the line dividing good and evil cuts through the heart of every human being.'
>
> Alexander Solzhenitsyn,
> *The Gulag Archipelago* (1973)

LORD OF THE FLIES

The novel Lord of the Flies *(1954) by William Golding takes as its premise the question of how people would act if liberated from the strictures and observation of society. It takes the situation of a group of young boys stranded without adults on an island and shows them descending into anarchy and cruelty. Golding took Hobbes' view of the natural 'bestial' nature of humankind. Zimbardo's experiment seemed to endorse it.*

Well-educated children regress to a murderously primitive state in Peter Brook's 1963 film adaptation of William Golding's Lord of the Flies.

A HAPPIER POSSIBILITY

Paul Bloom (b.1963) is a cognitive psychologist at Yale University. His experiments with babies as young as three months suggest that we might have an innate moral sense that leads us to prefer altruistic behaviour to obstructive and selfish behaviour. In working with very young children, direction and duration of gaze is used to indicate interest or preference. Bloom showed the babies an animation of a ball trying to go up a hill, then of a helpful square nudging it upwards and of an unhelpful triangle blocking its path. The babies greatly preferred the helpful square shape. He changed the helpful/unhelpful shapes and their colours to rule out aesthetic preference. He found that adding faces to the shapes strengthened the effect. Even the smallest babies preferred the helpful shapes, and they were too young to have learned about considerate and inconsiderate behaviour, so Bloom concluded that this showed an innate rudimentary moral sense.

The children in a 1961 study by the Canadian social psychologist Albert Bandura (b.1925) were old enough to know the difference between good and bad behaviour. He wanted to know whether they would follow a role model, good or bad, given the opportunity to do so, without risk of punishment. He and his colleagues at Stanford recruited 72 young children, with adult researchers to act as models, and acquired some Bobo dolls – large, durable inflatable dolls that can be knocked over but quickly spring back to an upright position.

He divided his 72 young subjects into groups who were exposed either to an adult behaving violently towards a Bobo doll, a non-aggressive role model who played normally with some toys, or no role model. The children later had unsupervised access to the Bobo doll.

Bandura found that children who had seen an aggressive role model were the most likely to abuse the Bobo doll themselves. The least aggressive children were those exposed to a non-aggressive role model, so that seemed to have a good influence (better than no role model at all). Seeing a male aggressive model was more likely to make boys aggressive; the gender of the role model made little difference to girls, except that if they saw a male aggressive role model the girls were more likely to be physically aggressive and if they saw a female aggressive role model they were more likely to be verbally aggressive.

There have been criticisms of the experiment. Would the effect have lasted longer than the few minutes of the experiment? Were the children trying to please the adults by copying their behaviour?

Bandura carried out a similar experiment in 1963 with children aged between two-and-a-half and six years old. He showed the children films in which a model aggressively attacked and screamed at a Bobo doll, and then was either rewarded with sweets, or punished with a warning. The children were then allowed to play in a room with a Bobo doll. Children who had seen the aggression rewarded were more likely to be aggressive themselves.

Variations on the Bobo doll experiment have consistently come up with much the same results. Modern brain scanning methods can add a physiological dimension to such experiments. In 2006, a study at the Indiana University School of Medicine carried out brain scans on 44 young people straight after they had played either a violent or a non-violent video game. Those who had played violent games showed extra activity in the amygdala, the part of the brain responsible for stimulating emotions. There was reduced activity in the prefrontal lobe, which regulates self-control, inhibition and concentration. Those who played non-violent games showed no such changes in brain activity. Studies such as this, showing a change in behaviour and brain activity common to several subjects, suggest there is a genuine mechanism at work in the mind that could be predictive of behaviour and might well be common to all people.

Follow the crowd

Most of us want to fit in to society to varying degrees. Even if we don't consciously want to conform, we quickly learn that life is a lot easier if we observe some social norms. A series of experiments in the mid-20th century explored the degree to which people want to conform, obey, fit in and generally not rock the boat. People are, it seems, more sheep-like than we expect.

Fitting in can sometimes be good, but it can also lead to horrific behaviour – as in the case of the Nazi atrocities. Another of the experiments that followed in the wake of World War II tested subjects' willingness to follow orders, even when those orders were to behave in unacceptable ways. Its results were shocking.

DARWIN'S BABY

Charles Darwin made detailed notes on the development of his son, William. He recorded that at two years and eight months, William showed signs of guilt and shame, hiding the stains on his clothes that showed he had stolen food. Darwin reported that the boy had never been punished, so he was not motivated by fear of the consequences.

Charles Darwin with his son William c.1842.

THE MILGRAM EXPERIMENT

In 1961, the American social psychologist Stanley Milgram (1933–84) recruited 40 volunteers to help with a study of learning at Yale, all of them men between the ages of 20 and 50 (so comparable to those who might have become concentration camp guards in Nazi Germany). He told them they would be randomly allocated roles as learners or teachers, but in fact they were all to be teachers and the 'students' were actors.

The 'teacher's' role was to ask questions of a 'student' seemingly strapped to a chair in another room and attached to two electrodes. He was told that if the student got a question wrong, he was to administer an electric shock. This started at a very mild level of 15 volts, but rose progressively to a maximum of 450 volts as the student gave more and more incorrect answers.

The teachers were given a script to follow, and strict instructions to administer shocks for wrong answers or silence. The student also had a script, and had to act out screaming, begging and writhing in their chairs as they were apparently subjected to more and more pain. At 300 volts, the student banged on the wall, begging to be let out; at higher levels of shock the student fell silent. The experimenter sat in the room

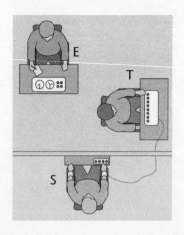

A diagram of Milgram's experiment. The experimenter ('E') tells the teacher ('T') to administer a series of electric shocks to the student ('S') who, unbeknown to the teacher, is an actor reading from a script.

with the teacher and encouraged him to carry on if he became reluctant. The teacher could hear but not see what was happening in the other room. The experimenter would urge the teacher to continue with the experiment but did not threaten or intimidate in any way.

'I set up a simple experiment at Yale University to test how much pain an ordinary citizen would inflict on another person simply because he was ordered to by an experimental scientist. Stark authority was pitted against the subjects' strongest moral imperatives against hurting others, and, with the subjects' ears ringing with the screams of the victims, authority won more often than not. The extreme willingness of adults to go to almost any lengths on the command of an authority constitutes the chief finding of the study and the fact most urgently demanding explanation.'

Stanley Milgram (1974)

'When you think of the long and gloomy history of man, you will find more hideous crimes have been committed in the name of obedience than have ever been committed in the name of rebellion.'

B. F. Skinner (1974)

In all, just under two-thirds (65 per cent) of Milgram's volunteers continued to the highest level of shock, 450 volts, and all reached 300 volts. Milgram concluded that we have an overwhelming urge to obey an authority figure.

CHAPTER 7

Milgram debriefed his volunteers, and explained the experiment to them. He found three types of subject:

- Some obeyed but sought to justify their actions. They shifted responsibility on to the experimenter or even the student (for being stupid).
- Some obeyed and blamed themselves. They felt bad about what they had done.
- A few rebelled, putting the student's well-being above the demands of the experiment.

Varying the experiment, Milgram found that obedience levels were higher when the experiment took place in a lab at the university, the experimenter wore a lab coat and stayed in the same room as the teacher. They were lower if the experiment was conducted in a run-down office in the city, the experimenter wore ordinary clothes and was in a different room. Subjects were also much more obedient if they didn't have to press the switch themselves but could delegate the task of administering the shock to an assistant.

Milgram suggested that we have two different states: autonomous and 'agentic'. In the autonomous state, we make our own choices and take responsibility for our actions, acting according to our own values and standards. In the agentic state, we carry out orders with no sense of personal responsibility. When faced with a figure of authority, he claimed, most people undergo an 'agentic shift' from the autonomous to the obedient state and this can explain any number of atrocities committed in the name of 'following orders'.

The validity of Milgram's results has been queried, and psychologist Gina Perry, author of *Behind the Shock Machine* (2013), found significant problems with both his method and his reporting. But it still seems that a fair proportion of people will take obedience far enough to inflict seemingly serious harm on another. It may not be that there is an inner-Nazi in all of us, but that there is an alarming tendency to do as we are told, even if we doubt the morality or wisdom of the order.

CROWD PLEASERS

The tendency to conform to expectations without even being given orders, or to blend in with the crowd, has been demonstrated by other experiments, too. In Zimbardo's Stanford Prison experiment, 'prisoners' applied for parole when they could just have left. Parents visiting played in role even though they had not agreed to be part of the study.

> 'Could it be that Eichmann and his million accomplices in the Holocaust were just following orders? Could we call them all accomplices?'
>
> Stanley Milgram (1974)

In 1951, the Polish social psychologist Solomon Asch (1907–96) investigated more benignly how far people will compromise themselves to conform. He placed a subject in a group with seven other people, and showed the group several pairs of cards.

> 'Ordinary people, simply doing their jobs, and without any particular hostility on their part, can become agents in a terrible destructive process. Moreover, even when the destructive effects of their work become patently clear,

> *and they are asked to carry out actions incompatible with fundamental standards of morality, relatively few people have the resources needed to resist authority.'*
>
> **Stanley Milgram (1974)**

> *'Now that I look back, I realize that a life predicated on being obedient and taking orders is a very comfortable life indeed. Living in such a way reduces to a minimum one's own need to think.'*
>
> **Nazi war criminal Adolf Eichmann (1960)**

In each pair, one card had a single line on it and the other had three lines of differing lengths, one of which matched the line on the first card. The participants had to say which of the three lines, labelled A, B and C, matched the single line. This exercise was repeated many times.

For the first set of trials, Asch's confederates gave the correct answer. Thereafter, they all agreed on the wrong answer – but they all gave their answers first, leaving the subject to respond last each time. Asch was interested to see whether volunteers would be swayed by the wrong answers given by others.

In a control experiment, a volunteer answered the questions alone and gave a wrong answer less than 1 per cent of the time, demonstrating that the task was easy.

However, when the confederates agreed on a wrong answer Asch found that 75 per cent of his subjects gave an incorrect answer at least once. Interviewed later, the participants who gave wrong answers fell into the three groups listed on the facing page.

Subjects in Asch's experiment had to say which line on the right-hand card matched the line on the left-hand card.

- They actually believed the incorrect answer was true.
- They thought they must be wrong because everyone else agreed (Asch called this a 'distortion of judgement').
- They realized that everyone else was giving the wrong answer, but didn't want to look inferior or be the odd one out (Asch called this a 'distortion of action').

Of those who did not give the wrong answer, even though it set them apart, some acted confidently, some acted in a withdrawn way and some showed doubt but stuck with the right answer. When he varied the experiment, he found that if a single other person gave the correct answer, or if people could record their answers in writing rather than saying them aloud, rates of conformity with the wrong answer fell.

SMOKE AND ACCIDENTS

Asch's experiment did not deal with a serious or threatening situation, but other experimenters have found high levels of conformity and reluctance to act independently even when that course of action produces danger. In New York in 1964, a woman called Kitty Genovese was attacked and murdered in front of 38 witnesses, none of whom (according to press reports at the time) came to her aid. The case sparked a significant psychological study into what was known as the 'bystander effect' – and which later came to be known also as 'Genovese syndrome'.

In 1968, American social psychologists John Darley (1938–2018) and Bibb Latané (b.1937) set up an experiment to discover whether people would help a stranger in distress. They recruited volunteers who were told they were going to take part in a psychological study about personal problems and that because the issues discussed were private, the discussion would take place over intercom systems and the participants couldn't see each other. Part way through a discussion, one participant (an actor) faked a seizure, becoming increasingly distressed and saying they felt they would die. Other participants could hear this – and each other – over the intercom.

Darley and Latané found that the more people were involved in the discussion, the less likely it was that they would help. Even though they could not see the other participants, they knew they were there. It seemed that each person felt they had less responsibility towards the stranger in distress because there were other people around who should also feel responsible. In contrast, when a participant was the only person involved, they sought help 85 per cent of the time.

Darley and Latané carried out another experiment, this time apparently putting the participants in danger. They set students to complete questionnaires in a room. After a while, smoke started to leak into the room. The smoke got thicker and thicker until the students could hardly see. If students were alone when the room filled with smoke, 75 per cent reported the problem. But if they were in a room with two other people who ignored the smoke only 10 per cent raised the alarm. We assume that other people know more than we do and so if they are not responding to a crisis, we don't need to either. Psychologists call it 'pluralistic ignorance'. We would rather risk death than embarrass ourselves by raising a false alarm.

JOIN THE GROUP

There is an overt desire for conformity and to be part of a group. This was studied in 1967, not by a psychologist but an American history teacher, Ron Jones (b.1941), in Palo Alto, California. Jones had difficulty convincing his high school students that fascism took root so quickly in Nazi Germany so he started a movement, which he called 'The Third Wave', with the aim of overthrowing democracy. He made a convincing case for a different system being better able to deliver a high standard of performance and so greater rewards for individuals. The problem with democracy, he said, is that because it focuses on the individual, it reduces the strength of the group.

'Strength through discipline, strength through community, strength through action, strength through pride.'

Motto of Jones' Third Wave group

Jones had intended to run the experiment for one day only, but it was so successful that he continued with it. He added more authoritarian trappings, including a salute and formal greetings that excluded non-members. Within three days, 200 students had joined and their academic performance had improved. Some started to denounce other members who broke any of the rules. On the fourth day, Jones felt it had got out of hand and would have to stop. He called the group to an assembly on the pretext that the national movement was about to be launched. Once they were gathered, he told them it had all been an experiment; then he showed them a film about the Third Reich.

As with Turner's theory of self-categorization, Jones' students were keen to define themselves in terms of the Third Wave group. They wanted to assimilate the values they thought the group represented and have them as part of their personal identity. But Jones has demonstrated quite effectively that we all want to belong, and easily become, in Adolf Eichmann's words, 'one of the many horses pulling the wagon', even if the wagon is on the way to hell.

Driven from within

The humanistic psychologists were more concerned with the empowerment of the individual than with group identity or what we all have in common. Yet on the path to self-actualization, we all have to meet other needs first, according to Abraham Maslow.

THE PYRAMID OF NEEDS

In 1954, Maslow published a diagram that explained his theory of human motivation. The 'pyramid of needs' shows the hierarchy of needs that must be met, in order, on the path to 'self-actualization'. These needs, he maintained, provide the motivation for all human endeavour. Although Maslow produced

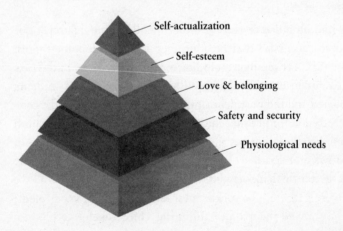

Self-actualization

Self-esteem

Love & belonging

Safety and security

Physiological needs

his pyramid as a kind of road map for personal development, it demonstrates the universal human condition. What makes us a member of the human race is the drive to satisfy these needs, and what marks us out as individuals is the self-actualization we achieve at the end of the process.

At the bottom of the pyramid are the most fundamental physical needs – the need for food, water, sleep, air and basic bodily functions. Once these are met, we try to meet the need for security – both physical safety and the security that comes from having a stable job, a house, and so on. Next, we can move on to the need for love and belonging, met by having family, friends and sexual intimacy. This is followed by the need for esteem and respect, including self-esteem and confidence. With that need met, we can move on to self-actualization (see pages 193–4).

Maslow recognized the baser needs and recommended meeting them, whereas many of his predecessors had said the needs should be suppressed, denied, or ignored in pursuit of higher ideals. For Maslow, the needs drive all human action and part of the human condition – a good, productive part, for they spur us on to achievement.

Inside and outside the group

We all want to be individuals and yet we all want to belong, to be part of the group and not excluded. Self-actualization, if it comes, might make us feel comfortable to be different. But there are dangers involved in being different. One of those dangers is being considered mad. Those who have tried to be different, or have not tried hard enough to be like everyone else, have often been marginalized, demonized, pathologized and institutionalized. The flipside of trying to determine what the human mind is like is the discovery that some people are different.

CHAPTER 8
Approaches to abnormal psychology

'I have of late, but wherefore I know not, lost all my mirth, forgone all custom of exercises; and indeed, it goes so heavily with my disposition that this goodly frame, the earth, seems to me a most sterile promontory... why it appeareth nothing to me but a foul and pestilent congregation of vapours... Man delights me not; nor woman neither.'

William Shakespeare, Hamlet (Act 1, Scene 3)

The Hungarian-born psychiatrist Thomas Szasz (1920–2012) suggested that people often have difficulties in life because they are not trying to live to the same pattern as the rest of us. They are the ones who have been classified as mad, disturbed, or mentally ill.

Madness is in the eye of the beholder – the 'mad' are not like us, and that's what makes us regard them as mad. There are now several ways of defining abnormal psychology that take account of criteria such as whether the person can function adequately in society, whether they are in distress, and how far they stray from 'normal' levels of mental health.

What's wrong with you?

As with physical illness, people can suffer acute episodes of mental illness or have a long-term, chronic psychiatric condition. Some people are born with minds that are different from the norm, just as some are born with bodies that are different, or mental problems can develop over time. This has been explained in three different ways: the supernatural (demons or spirits did it), the biological (there is a physical cause), and the psychological (mental events or conditions lie behind it).

In the absence of any better idea, mental illness has often been blamed on gods, spirits or demons. Even some of the otherwise enlightened Ancient Greeks and Romans blamed madness on the action of the gods. After the fall of the Roman Empire around AD400, all physiological and psychological approaches to madness were forgotten and people reverted to superstition. By the early Middle Ages, the intellectual centre shifted to the Arabic and Persian world, where classical writings were translated and augmented. Middle Eastern doctors generally followed the Greek physician Galen in attributing mental distress to an imbalance of the humours (see pages 159–61). For example, Ibn Sina considered that bestial madness, characterized by confusion, agitation, ferocity and behaving like a predatory animal, was caused by burnt yellow or black bile reaching the brain.

MOONSTRUCK

The word 'lunacy' originates with the Roman belief that some madness was caused by the influence of the moon or the action of the moon goddess, Luna.

But non-academic Arabs continued to believe that madness was mainly due to supernatural factors, such as jinn (evil spirits or 'genies'). Indeed the Arab word for madness, junun, means possession by jinn. It could also be caused by the evil eye, by failing to observe rituals and taboos, by God, by non-supernatural means such as trauma, or by heredity.

EPILEPSY – THE SACRED DISEASE

Epilepsy is now considered a neurological disorder, but for millennia its symptoms – seizures, loss of consciousness, drooling – were considered a sign of madness.

The earliest account of epilepsy is from Mesopotamia, written 4,000 years ago. The patient was said to be under the influence of a moon god and was exorcized. In the Babylonian Code of Hammurabi, written around 1790BC, if a person bought a slave who was then discovered to have epilepsy they could return him and get a refund. The condition was considered to be the result of evil spirits possessing the patient and was treated by supernatural means. The Ancient Greeks associated epilepsy with good spirits and genius – they called it the 'sacred disease'. Hippocrates was a dissenting voice, saying that it was a physical disease in which heredity plays a part, but for once his views did not prevail. An association between epilepsy and spirits persisted into the 17th century in Europe. In Tanzania today, epilepsy is still considered to be caused by witchcraft or possession by evil spirits.

In Europe, encouraged by the Christian Church, with its panoply of demons and evil spirits, supernatural explanations of madness prevailed until the Enlightenment. Treatment of mentally ill people was often inhumane, the abuse intended to drive out the evil spirits assaulting or possessing them. The mentally ill were sometimes tortured and executed during the witch-hunts that claimed many lives in Europe and America between the 15th and 18th centuries. Displaying strange but harmless behaviours, such as mumbling, raving and repetitive actions, could be enough to bring a charge of witchcraft and death by hanging or burning.

'If you talk to God, you are praying; If God talks to you, you have schizophrenia. If the dead talk to you, you are a spiritualist; If you talk to the dead, you are a schizophrenic.'
                                                        Thomas Szasz (1973)

BAD MAD WORDS

We no longer say people are mad. Some people now prefer the term 'mental distress', avoiding the stigma of illness. The past had no such sensibilities. Visitors paid one penny to see 'lunatics' – they did not pay to see 'mentally distressed people'. In the early part of the 20th century, the terms 'idiot', 'imbecile' and 'moron' had precise medical meanings. An idiot was someone with an IQ of 0–20; an imbecile had an IQ of 21–50; and a moron had an IQ of 51–70.

But where there are bad spirits there can also be good spirits. Just as the Greeks considered epilepsy sacred, so some forms of apparent madness were considered to be divine inspiration or the presence of the Holy Ghost. In the 16th century, the Moorish author and historian Joannes Leo Africanus (1494–1554) wrote that in North Africa, 'There are certain people . . . whom a man would take to be distraughte, which goe bare-headed and bare-footed, carrying stones about with them, and these are reverenced by the common people, for men of singular holiness.'

A HISTORY OF HYSTERIA

Hysteria is now known as histrionic personality disorder (HPD). It is characterized by excessive displays of emotion, attention-seeking, inappropriate sexual displays or behaviour, self-dramatizing and theatrical behaviour, being easily impressed, manipulative, egocentric, often emotionally shallow and changeable. It affects 2–3 per cent of the general population in the USA. More women than men are diagnosed with it.

The Ancient Egyptians were the first to mention hysteria. In the Ebers papyrus, dating from 1900BC, it is linked with the uterus. The Ancient Greeks perpetuated this belief; Hippocrates, who was the first to use the term hysteria,

said that it was caused by wayward movement of the uterus (hysteron) due to too little sexual activity. It was not until the 17th century that the uterus was let off the hook. The English physician Thomas Willis (1621–75) suggested that the brain and nervous system were at the root of hysteria, and that meant that men could also suffer from it.

The German physician Franz Mesmer (1734–1815) treated patients with hysteria using his technique of mesmerism, a form of suggestion. In the 19th century Jean-Martin Charcot used hypnosis with his hysteric patients. Charcot influenced Freud, who accounted for hysteria by saying that it occurs when the individual's libido does not evolve as it should do. There has been some suggestion recently that HPD is not a psychological disorder at all but a kind of cultural disorder. By this account, people diagnosed with HPD are being so labelled because they don't conform to the prevailing behavioural norms rather than because they have a mental condition.

MARGERY KEMPE (*c*.1373–1440)

The English mystic Margery Kempe wrote the first memoir or autobiography in English. She seems to have suffered some form of mental illness after the birth of her first child, perhaps post-natal depression or mania, as she records that she believed she was surrounded by demons. She also resorted to self-harm. Later, after experiencing a religious vision, she would frequently roar and rage in church, believing this to be the influence of the Holy Ghost. The Church appears to have agreed with her, as she was allowed to go on pilgrimages and sometimes encouraged to go to church and experience her 'visitations' without being accused of witchcraft or unnatural behaviour.

Biology and the brain

Hippocrates dismissed supernatural accounts of illness. He taught that there are physical causes, most commonly an imbalance of the four humours, that could affect mood and behaviour as well as having physical effects. He made an exception for hysteria (see panel on pages 222–3).

A MIND UNBALANCED

The Greek physician Asclepiades of Bithynia (c.127–40BC) dismissed humoral theory as the cause of psychological distress, laying the blame on emotional problems. So did the Swiss physician and alchemist Paracelsus (1493–1541), who thought a chemical imbalance was responsible, as he was able to treat his patients using herbal preparations. He saw the body as a chemical system that must be kept in balance with itself (the 'microcosm'), and with the larger environment (the 'macrocosm').

Paracelsus divided mental problems into five classes:

- epilepsy
- mania
- *chorea lasciva* (lascivious behaviour)

- *suffocatio intellectus* (suffocation of the intellect)
- true insanity (those permanently insane with no periods of lucidity or remission)

He said that epilepsy is caused by the *spiritus vitae* (spirit of life) boiling and rising to the brain. He recommended a herbal remedy in cases that were not entrenched, but said sometimes epilepsy is present from birth (a view he shared with Hippocrates). Mania he ascribed to some kind of humour that rises up the body and collects in the head, where part of it condenses and part remains as a vapour.

Neither *chorea lasciva* nor *suffocatio intellectus* is clearly described. He mentions three types of *suffocatio intellectus*: one is caused by intestinal worms, one afflicts only women and is caused by malfunction of the womb (presumably hysteria), and another is a sleep disorder. He also cites several causes of *chorea lasciva* including recklessness and disgraceful living:

> *'Thus, the cause of the disease chorea lasciva is a mere opinion and idea, assumed by imagination, affecting those who believe in such a thing. This opinion and idea are the origin of the disease both in children and adults. In children the case is also imagination, based not on thinking but on perceiving, because they have heard or seen something. The reason is this: their sight and hearing are so strong that unconsciously they have fantasies about what they have seen or heard.'*

Paracelsus gave a taxonomy of mental illness that also included five 'true insanities'. These were melancholy (depression); lunacy caused by the moon; permanent insanity caused by eating or drinking (something poisonous, presumably); those who were born insane, either because they inherited insanity from a parent or because the 'seed' was defective; and, finally, those who are possessed by demons. This is the only mention he makes of demonic possession and he doesn't elaborate upon it.

WORKING WITH HUMOURS

Paracelsus was something of a maverick. Most people who sought a physical source of mental distress followed humoral theory, even in the 19th century. Humoral theory gave a way of categorizing mental disorders by aetiology, or cause. So depression (melancholy) resulted from an excess of black bile. Consequently, treatments were aimed at reducing the preponderance of black bile, usually by purging and bleeding the patient.

The methods of diagnosing humoral imbalance included listening to the patient's own account of their troubles and daily life, and examining and even tasting the blood and urine to determine the type of humoral imbalance.

THE ANATOMY OF MELANCHOLY

The first full-length textbook on depression, The Anatomy of Melancholy, *was published in 1621 by the English scholar Richard Burton (1577–1640). It is an encyclopaedic tome that ran to 900 pages in its first edition, and Burton continued to extend it throughout his life. The style is arcane and rambling; it is stuffed with classical quotations and references and covers myriad topics only slightly related to depression. Even so, Burton distinguished between routine misery caused by life events ('reactive depression', as it would be called now) and entrenched melancholy ('clinical depression', in modern terms). He described 'Melancholy in disposition' rather long-windedly as:*

'...transitory Melancholy which goes and comes upon every small occasion of sorrow, need, sickness, trouble, fear, grief, passion, or perturbation of the mind, any manner of care, discontent, or thought, which causes anguish, dulness, heaviness and vexation of spirit, any ways opposite to pleasure, mirth, joy, delight, causing forwardness in us, or a dislike...'

The other type of melancholy (clinical depression) is 'melancholy of habit' and is the main subject of his book:

'This Melancholy of which we are to treat, is a habit, a serious ailment, a settled humour, as Aurelianus and others call it, not errant, but fixed: and as it was long increasing, so...it will hardly be removed.'

'The melancholike man . . . is afraid of everything . . . he would runne away and cannot goe . . . he is become as a savadge creature haunting the shadowed places, suspicious, solitarie, enemie to the sunne, and one whom nothing can please, but only discontentment, which forgeth unto itselfe a thousand false and vain imaginations.'
Anatomist Andreas Laurentius (1558–1609)

THE BRAIN REVEALED

Eventually a link began to emerge between the physical state of the brain and some forms of mental disturbance. The most striking case study was that of railroad worker Phineas Gage.

Gage suffered a terrible accident in 1848 when working as a construction foreman on the railroads in Vermont, USA. A tamping iron – a long, pointed metal rod – was fired accidentally through his head, entering his skull through the cheek, leaving through the top of his head, and destroying much of the left frontal lobe of his brain on the way. The stalwart Gage apparently sat upright in an ox-cart for the journey to town, and chatted helpfully to his doctor. Gage was not expected to live and yet made a miraculous recovery. But he is said to have suffered a personality change, becoming offensive and rude. Although there are conflicting reports, these changes seem to have been temporary.

Contemporary psychologists seized on Gage as an example, although his case did not show much that was conclusive except, perhaps, that removal of the frontal lobe need not be fatal. He was used as an illustration by phrenologists in support of their theories that the Organ of Veneration and/or the Organ of Benevolence was destroyed and this accounted for his subsequent rude behaviour (but not for the fact that it corrected itself over time). He was also used to demonstrate that there is no localization of function in the brain, as he was later capable of doing pretty much everything he could do before – even with most of the left frontal lobe missing. Clearly, these two conclusions are mutually exclusive.

The theory of localization of brain function gained apparent support in 1861. The French surgeon Paul Pierre Broca (1824–80) discovered an area of the brain, now known as Broca's area, that is responsible for speech. Broca's discovery came about when he carried out a post-mortem on a patient, Leborgne, who had lost the ability to speak and could say only one word, 'tan'. Broca found a lesion in the frontal lobe of the brain caused by syphilis. A second patient, Lelong, could say only five words; Broca found the same area of the frontal lobe was damaged.

Since then, more areas of the brain responsible for particular functions have been discovered. Modern imaging methods such as PET scans and MRI scans have been used to show which areas are at work when particular tasks are performed and to compare the sizes of structures in different brains (see pages 100–101). The abnormal size or level of activity of part of the brain is sometimes implicated in particular types of abnormal psychology. Further, DNA sequencing has turned up links between some gene variations and abnormal psychology.

All in the mind

The first thorough approach to psychological causes came with the work of Sigmund Freud and the Austrian physician Joseph Breuer (1842–1925). According to Freud, all disturbances in the adult mind are the result of past trauma, usually originating in childhood, that has been forgotten or repressed. His theory was that previous physical and mental or emotional experiences produce our mental states and that after deep conversation with a therapist who 'analyzes' the patient, the problem can be brought to the surface and defused.

THE IMPORTANCE OF SEX

Freud decided that all neurosis stems from an incident in childhood that involves sexual abuse ('seduction', usually by an adult). Early in his career, he claimed that he had uncovered such sexual episodes in all his patients. Much later, he changed his tune and said that the sexual abuse did not necessarily happen, but was present as a memory or a fantasy in each patient and that had the same effect. In fact, none of his patients had recalled any instance of childhood sexual abuse prior to their treatment.

Freud regarded every aspect of human behaviour as being driven by libido, which he considered specifically a sexual drive.

Many of his most influential and erudite followers parted company with him because he placed sex at the centre of all his work. Most felt, not unreasonably, that there could be other drives and incidents that affected behaviour and mental health. Carl Jung and Alfred Adler were the most famous of the defectors. One psychologist who stuck by him throughout was his daughter, Anna Freud.

THE KILLER WITHIN?

The American neuroscientist James Fallon (b.1947) made a particularly striking discovery in 2006. While studying brain scans of psychopaths and, separately, Alzheimer's patients, he discovered that his own brain matched the profile he had developed of psychopathic brains. (He had used his own brain scan as a control in the Alzheimer's study.) It had lower than normal levels of activity in areas of the frontal and temporal lobes associated with empathy. When he looked at genetic indicators, he found he also had a variant of the MAO-A gene linked with psychopathy. Investigating his family history, Fallon found that he was related to several convicted murderers, and the notorious Lizzie Borden, accused (but acquitted) of murdering her parents with an axe in 1892. He concluded that he is a pro-social psychopath: ambitious, high-achieving, but not dangerous. A different upbringing, though, might have turned him into a full-blown serial killer.

FREUD'S PROBLEMS WITH SEX

Psychosexual stages: Freud believed that all children go through stages in their early development when they gain sexual pleasure from different areas of the body, called erogenous zones. During the first year, the oral stage, the erogenous zone is the mouth. The baby gains pleasure from suckling and exploring objects with his or her mouth. During the next year, the erogenous zone is the anus as the baby learns bowel control. From the ages of two to five, the genitals are the erogenous zone. Freud called this the phallic stage, which he applied to boys and girls as he considered the clitoris a type of mini-penis. Arrested development in any of these stages could, he believed, lead to particular types of personality or disorder. Freud focused on three aspects of the developing mind as especially significant:

Oedipus complex: Children of both genders, Freud claimed, develop an intense sexual attraction towards their mothers during the phallic stage. In boys, this Oedipus complex grows into competition with the father for the mother's affection and the fantasy (latent, at least) of killing the father and replacing him. The name is taken from the Greek legend of Oedipus.

Castration anxiety: The boy sees his father as more powerful than himself and as the source of his feelings towards his mother is his penis, he develops castration anxiety – he is afraid his powerlessness will be physically manifested.

Penis envy: The girl notices her father possesses something valuable – a penis – which she does not have. She envies him this, but as she can't have it, she 'becomes' her mother and shares him instead.

DISSENTING VOICES

The German–American psychologist Hugo Münsterberg (1863–1916) studied many people with mental illness in his attempts to understand the causes of abnormal behaviour. He had no patience with Freud's psychoanalytic approach, though, and made no attempt to investigate a patient's past or unconscious motivation. Instead, he encouraged patients to expect an improvement in their condition and believed that improvement would then follow. He considered genuine psychosis to be untreatable, as he thought it was caused by degenerative damage to the nervous system and so was a physiological rather than psychological problem.

The behaviourist John B. Watson also saw mental illness as the result of early experiences, but not through undergoing a process of internalization and festering, as Freud would have it. Watson argued that many of the so-called symptoms of so-called mental illness were conditioned reflexes in which the conditioning was counterproductive. He was interested in particular psychoanalytic tools, such as word association tests, which he thought could allow one to trace the origins and precise nature of the twisted habits that manifested as mental illness.

MOVING ON

Although some of Freud's work has been discredited, the idea that early experiences leave a lasting impression and affect later psychological states is now rarely disputed. Freud's one-time colleague Adler developed his own theory, that feelings of inferiority or superiority arose in childhood. Today, a massive psychotherapy industry is based around the general premise that how one is treated as a child and later life experiences can have a lasting and sometimes damaging effect on the psyche.

Counting the ways

In the 2nd century BC, Asclepiades of Bithynia distinguished between acute and chronic psychological disorders and between hallucinations and delusions. An acute episode could occur after bereavement or other loss; the depression would pass as they adjusted to their loss. A chronic condition could be permanent insanity or unremitting mood disorder.

The Roman author Aulus Cornelius Celsus (*c.*25BC–*c.*AD50) provided the earliest use of the term insanity (or 'insania') in his *De medicina*, written around AD30. He distinguished between the different types by the patient's behaviour:

> '*There are several sorts of insanity; for some among insane persons are sad, others hilarious; some are more readily controlled and rave in words only, others are rebellious and act with violence; and of these latter, some only do harm by impulse, others are artful too, and show the most complete appearance of sanity while seizing occasion for mischief, but they are detected by the result of their acts.*'

Celsus gave accounts of people who thought they were gods, famous figures, inanimate objects, or animals; of epilepsy and of paranoia; and distinguished between the hallucinations caused by fever and genuine delusions.

The Roman medical philosopher Aretaeus (AD50–130) recognized the pattern of bipolar disorder: periods of depression alternating with periods of mania or excitability, with periods of lucidity in between. He campaigned for humane treatment of the mentally ill, realizing that it was not only those of limited intelligence who can have mental health problems.

In the 10th century, the Arabian physician Najab ud-din Muhammad identified 30 different types of mental illness, including agitated depression, neurosis, sexual impotence, psychosis, schizophrenia, mania, priapism, obsessive-compulsive disorders, delusional disorders and degenerative diseases.

The Swiss physician Felix Platter (1536–1614) outlined several different types of mental disorder including mania, delirium, hallucinations, foolishness and obsessive unwelcome thoughts (which would now be considered an aspect of OCD, Obsessive Compulsive Disorder).

> '[In cases of melancholy,] imagination and judgement are so perverted that without any cause the victims become very sad and fearful. For they cannot adduce any certain cause of grief or fear except a trivial one or a false opinion which they have conceived as a result of disturbed apprehension...This frightful melancholy, which often drives men to despair, is the most common form of melancholy. In curing it I have been frequently very much impeded. They have often confessed to me with many tears and deep sighs, with the greatest anguish of heart and with their whole body trembling that, when seized by this, they have felt themselves driven toward blaspheming God and committing many horrible things, toward laying violent hands on themselves, killing their husbands or wives or children or neighbours or rulers, not out of motives of jealousy and not out of envy toward them, whom rather they fondly love, but out of an involuntary compulsion. They say that such thoughts creep up on them against their will and that they continually and urgently call upon God to deign to free them from such impious thoughts.'
>
> Felix Platter (1602)

FROM SYMPTOMS TO SYNDROMES

The first thorough attempt at classification came in the 19th century. The German psychiatrist Emil Kraepelin (1856–1926) studied psychology with Wundt. He wanted to categorize mental disorders as thoroughly as Wundt had categorized sensations, and to that end he spent years studying patients with mental disorders, determining the course, outcome and prognosis of different conditions. As with physical illness, the same symptoms can have many different causes. It is no more sensible to assume that everyone suffering hallucinations has the same mental condition as that everyone sneezing has the same physical illness.

Before Kraepelin, doctors had listed the symptoms of several hundred forms of mental illness, but he took a different approach, which he called clinical. Instead of grouping together cases that shared major symptoms, Kraepelin used patterns of symptoms, or syndromes, as the basis of his classification system.

One of his most important contributions was to divide mental illness into two categories. The first he called 'manic–depressive psychosis' (now called bipolar disorder), which recurs at regular intervals. The second he called 'dementia praecox' (premature dementia), because it usually appeared in early adulthood, it never went away and was degenerative. It was first described by the French physician Philippe Pinel (1745–1826) in the late 18th century. It was renamed schizophrenia in 1908 by the Swiss psychiatrist Paul Eugen Bleuler (1857–1939) when he determined that the dementia was a secondary symptom and decline did not always occur.

Kraepelin pioneered psychopharmacology – studying the effect of drugs on the nervous system – researching the impact of substances including morphine, coffee and alcohol. He expected that there would be a physical or genetic marker for all conditions, though these were not then known. An unfortunate consequence of his conviction that many mental disorders had genetic origins was that he was a supporter of eugenics, feeling the world would be a better place if these 'problems' were allowed to die out through restricted breeding.

The categorization of mental disorders undertaken by Kraepelin inspired the *Diagnostic and Statistical Manual* (DSM), which is used now by many psychiatrists to diagnose patients with mental problems. With increasing understanding of the structure, chemistry and biological processes of the brain, some mental health problems can now be explained more precisely – but not necessarily cured.

> **NEUROSIS AND PSYCHOSIS**
>
> *Psychosis involves losing touch with reality. Some mental illnesses are marked by periods of psychosis between long or short periods of lucidity. A few people are permanently out of touch with reality. Neurosis is an exaggerated response or concern with some aspect of living that causes anxiety, distress or obsession.*

Care, cure and containment

Mental disturbance can range from neurosis that disrupts a person's daily life to full-blown psychosis that makes them incapable of normal life. Clearly these require different types of treatment, though the treatment of mental distress always has been – and remains – difficult and often unsuccessful. In an ideal world, doctors could offer a cure. But more often, care or – at worst – containment has been the only provision for those with mental health problems. Many people in mental distress have been left untreated and either cared for by their families or left to wander from place to place, vulnerable and dependent on the goodwill of others. No doubt many came to a premature sticky end.

DEALING WITH DEMONS

The best way to counter something with supernatural causes was often thought to be by supernatural means, such as incantations, talismans and prayers. Sometimes, the supernatural methods

The Extraction of the Stone of Madness *by Hieronymous Bosch (c.1494).*

would appear to work as the person got better (whether by coincidence or suggestion), so reinforcing belief in the supernatural cause and cure. But treatment was not always as benign as using an incantation or talisman – it could be brutally physical, even in its supernatural aims.

The oldest known treatment is trephination. The 'surgeon' would bore a hole, or cut out a portion of the skull, using a knife or drill made of animal bone, shell, rock or metal. Trephination could have been used to treat headaches or fits, or to release spirits. The earliest surviving trephined skulls are Neolithic – about 10,000 years old. Around two-thirds show evidence of bone regrowth, showing that the patient survived for a considerable time. Some have been trephined repeatedly. Trephination is not limited to the distant past. The French physician Arnaldus de Villanova

(1235–1313) advocated trephination to let both demons and bad humours escape from the brain, and the practice is still used in some parts of Africa, South America and Melanesia.

An Ancient Greek suffering from mental or physical health problems in the 4th century BC might choose to visit a temple dedicated to the medical god Asclepius. He or she would first offer prayers and sacrifices and then sleep in a dormitory (a practice known as 'incubation'), hoping to be visited by dreams that would guide the priest/physician towards suitable treatment. Non-venomous snakes slithered freely around the floor of the dormitory, and were used in healing rituals – hence the snake in the snake-and-staff emblem, the Rod of Asclepius (the Greek God of healing), that has come to be associated with medicine. The physician's job was to interpret the patient's dreams correctly. Treatment might include medication with herbs, special diet, baths, massage or other physical treatments.

In the medieval Arab world, treatment was often enlightened, but could also include exorcism and cautery (burning) applied to parts of the body. In 13th century Anatolia, exorcisms were performed by dervishes. In Europe, too, exorcisms might have been attempted to save a person infested with demons – if they were not simply categorized as a witch and quickly despatched.

Getting physical

Physical treatments for mental illness rely on there being some kind of connection between ghost and machine. The predominant model throughout European history has been some attempt to rebalance the humours.

HUMOURING THE HUMOURS

With the Ancient Greeks, humoral theory led to some gentle and some invasive physical therapies. Many of the treatments Hippocrates recommended could have been beneficial: a healthy diet, lots of sleep, a regime of exercise and activity, pleasant baths and other gentle types of therapy. Others were less pleasant and probably less beneficial. Over the next two millennia, much harm was done through excessive blood-letting and purging.

Asclepiades of Bithynia, in the 2nd century BC, argued for sympathetic treatment of the mentally ill. He disapproved of bleeding, and of locking away people who were disturbed. Instead, he promoted natural treatments such as massage, diet and music therapy, with different styles of music recommended for patients with different mental states. He also advocated a swinging hammock to soothe distressed patients to sleep. The early Arab hospitals provided a combination of pleasant and unpleasant treatments for the mentally ill according to what was suitable for the patient's condition. This could be emetics, bleeding with cups or leeches, and baths. These treatments countered the excess of bile in the brain, either by removing it from the body (bleeding and emetics) or by diluting it (supplying extra moisture).

Paracelsus didn't follow the humoral model, but for all that some of his treatments were distinctly unpleasant. For mania, he suggested two treatments, one of which is barbaric, involving skinning of the fingers and toes (or other parts) either chemically or surgically so that the 'vapours' can escape. The alternative consists of taking medicines, and we can imagine would have been more popular with patients. *Chorea lasciva*, which he considered characterized by lascivious behaviour, he treated first by shutting the patient in a dark room with little food or water. If that didn't work, a sound beating was called for, and finally – for the most intransigent cases – he recommended throwing the patient into cold water.

Many of the brutal treatments inflicted on patients in madhouses and asylums from the 17th to 19th centuries were intended to help rebalance the humours, including blood-letting, purging (using emetics), starvation diets, and enforced cold baths. With the rise of institutions to house the mentally ill, it became possible to impose these treatments in a systematic and methodical way on large numbers of people.

> 'If, however, it is the mind that deceives the madman, he is best treated by certain tortures. When he says or does anything wrong, he is to be coerced by starvation, fetters and flogging. He is to be forced both to fix his attention and to learn something and to memorize it; for thus it will be brought about that little by little he will be forced by fear to consider what he is doing. To be terrified suddenly and to be thoroughly frightened is beneficial in this illness.'
>
> Celsus, 2nd century AD

HOSPITALS FOR THE MENTALLY ILL

One of the greatest achievements of medieval Islam was the founding of hospitals. No one was turned away on account of their inability to pay, and hospitals were open to both men and women.

The earliest firm evidence of a hospital making provision for the mentally ill is from Cairo, Egypt, in AD872 by Ahmad ibn Tulun, the Abbasid governor of Egypt. Many more followed, and it became standard practice for Islamic hospitals to provide for the mentally ill. In 1183, the traveller Ibn Jubayr described the Nasiri hospital in Cairo:

> 'A third [building]...is a large place, having rooms with iron windows; it serves as a place of confinement for the insane. They also have persons who daily examine their condition and give them what is fitting for them.'

There were tranquilizing medicines, such as opium, and calming music and massage. The intention was clearly care and cure, though he did later report that a hospital in Damascus had 'a system of treatment for confined lunatics, and they are bound in chains', apparently to protect the medical staff and patients. Some talking therapy, too, seems to have been current. The Persian physician Abu Bakr Mohammad Ibn Zakariya al-Razi (AD865–925), known in the West as 'Rhazes', advised doctors to help patients drive trifling matters about which they obsessed from their minds and build up their reasonable thoughts. Music, dramatic performances or readings, and prayer were also available to the patients.

Humane treatment in Islamic mental hospitals continued for many centuries. The Turkish travel writer Evliya Çelebi (1611–c.1682) recorded his visit to a hospital next to the Bayezid Mosque in Edirne, Turkey. He described a type of olfactory therapy with flowers, and remarked that a troupe of singers and musicians visited three times a week to play to the patients.

While in Arab countries mentally ill people could receive hospital treatment, in Europe those without family support wandered from place to place, begging for food.

Then, towards the end of the Middle Ages, a few small Christian institutions such as monasteries began to care for – or at least keep – the mentally ill along with paupers and the physically sick. People who could not care for a mentally ill relative could turn to the parish for help. The parish might provide a nurse, or board the mentally ill person in a special boarding house. Over time, these grew into private madhouses.

BEDLAM

The Priory of Saint Mary of Bethlehem, founded in 1247, is now better known as Bedlam. Originally a hospital for paupers, it began to take in mentally ill patients and by 1403 had six patients classified as insane. There were four pairs of manacles, eleven chains, six locks and two pairs of stocks that could have been used to restrain patients. By 1460, it had made the transition to being purely a mental hospital. For some centuries, Bedlam was run by 'keepers' with no particular medical knowledge or interest and who used the position for personal profit.

BOOMING BUSINESS

During the 17th century, the number of private madhouses grew rapidly. Many, Bedlam included, opened to the public, and viewing the 'lunatics' became a tourist attraction. At a charge of a penny a time, it was an important source of revenue. The conditions for inmates were often appalling. Many were kept permanently shackled, chained to walls, often lying on straw in their own filth, starving and freezing, with few or no clothes or bed-coverings. There were at the time 21 inmates, none of whom had been there for less than a year; one had been an inmate for 25 years.

Medical interventions included bleeding, beating and immersion in cold water. The gyrating chair, invented in the 18th century, was used to whirl the patient around at up to 100 revolutions a minute. It could be used in darkness for extra effect. The idea was to shake up the blood and tissues and restore equilibrium but it actually resulted in loss of consciousness and sometimes bleeding from the ears, nose and mouth.

In 1815, the case of a patient called James Norris brought conditions in Bedlam and other mental hospitals to public notice and an inquiry eventually led to the reform of madhouses.

'Some rooms are heated in winter according to the nature of the sick. . . . Those brought to the asylum by the police

> *are fettered by gilded and silver chains around their necks.*
> *Each one roars and sleeps like a lion in his lair. Some fix*
> *their eyes on the pool and the fountain and repeat words*
> *like a begging dervish. And some doze in the rose garden,*
> *grape orchards and fruit orchards . . . and sing with the*
> *unmelodious voices of the mad.'*
>
> Evliya Çelebi
> *Book of Travels*

A BETTER WAY: FROM MADHOUSE TO ASYLUM

Reform movements in the 18th and 19th centuries sought to put an end to the worst excesses in the madhouses. New methods, pioneered by the Italian physician Vincenzo Chiarugi (1759–1820), the English physician William Tuke (1732–1822) in England and Philippe Pinel in France, treated patients humanely. They were not chained or beaten, and did not have to work. If restraint were necessary, straitjackets or fabric bands reinforced with metal were used, rather than shackles. These were not madhouses but asylums, intended for care and, where possible, cure. The activist Dorothea Dix (1802–87) campaigned (successfully) for similar reforms in America in the mid-19th century.

> *'It is a supreme moral duty and medical obligation to*
> *respect the insane individual as a person.'*
> Vincenzo Chiarugi, *On Insanity* (1793–94)

Philippe Pinel, physician at the Bicêtre Hospital in Paris in 1793, worked with the unofficial governor, a former patient called Jean-Baptiste Pussin, to 'enrich the medical theory of mental illness with all the insights that the empirical approach affords'. They replaced bleeding, purging, and blistering with close personal contact and careful observation. His patients were unchained and Pinel engaged in long conversations with them. The method was clearly psychiatric. Pinel constructed detailed case histories that helped him to categorize different types of mental illness.

THE AGE OF ASYLUMS

The work begun by Chiarugi, Tuke and Pinel wrought a sea-change in the way the mentally ill were cared for. The 19th century saw dramatic social changes in Europe and America. Cities grew rapidly, and lifestyles changed. Vast, stately asylums sprung up to care for the mentally ill who could no longer be cared for by their families. The new asylums were built on a grand scale:

> 'Conceive a spacious building . . . airy, and elevated, and elegant, surrounded by extensive and swelling grounds and gardens. The interior is fitted up with galleries, and workshops, and music-rooms . . . all is clean, quiet and attractive.'

The ideal was to restore people to health by gentle methods, but the reality fell far short. Mentally ill people were removed entirely from their families because it was thought the best chance of cure came with 'removing the lunatic from all his habitual pastimes, distancing [him] from his place of residence, separating him from his family...surrounding him with strangers, altering his whole way of life' (French psychiatrist Jean-Etienne Esquirol, 1772–1842). Rigorous 'treatments' continued, or resurfaced, including bleeding, purging, and cold baths and showers.

The number of inmates increased by a factor of ten over the course of the 19th century and, by 1890, the asylums had sunk again into deplorable conditions. They were overcrowded and had returned to using straitjackets, seclusion and sedative drugs such as bromide to control disruptive or combative patients. Most people admitted to an asylum stayed there until they died. Again, reformers began to speak out against the asylums, and again conditions in the asylums fell until, in the second half of the 20th century, many were closed, putting responsibility for care back on the community.

Brave new treatments

The mental hospitals continued to fill up through the 19th and 20th centuries. In the first half of the 20th century, optimistic faith in science led to a clutch of radical treatments for mental illness. Patients were subjected to invasive and often experimental procedures including massive doses of insulin, electric shock treatment (later known as electroconvulsive therapy, ECT), prefrontal lobotomy, raising the body temperature to 41°C, or putting patients into a drug-induced sleep for days or weeks at a time.

ECT was introduced in 1938 by Italian neuropsychiatrists Ugo Cerletti (1877–1963) and Lucio Bini (1908–64). It consists of passing an electric current through the brain, causing convulsions. Relief of symptoms are said to be considerable after 10–20 treatments, which are usually given twice or three times a week. Drugs to induce convulsions had been used previously, with the first reported use in the 16th century, when convulsions were thought to reduce symptoms in severely depressed and schizophrenic patients. ECT as it was first given could result in broken arms and legs as the patients thrashed around, but was later administered with muscle relaxants and anaesthetic. ECT declined when better drug treatments for depression and schizophrenia emerged in the 1950s. Its waning popularity was accelerated by its negative portrayal in the 1962 novel and 1975 movie *One Flew Over the Cuckoo's Nest,* as well as by uncertainty surrounding its medical effects.

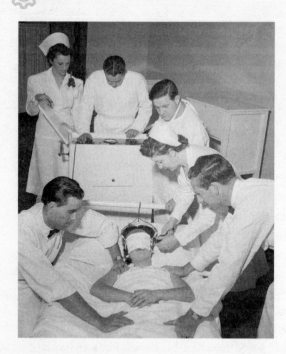

Electroshock therapy, c.1942.

Prefrontal lobotomy was another experimental method inflicted on many unsuspecting and unconsenting patients. It involves destroying much of the connection to the prefrontal lobe of the brain. The technique was first found to make chimpanzees docile; three months after this result had been reported, the Portuguese neurologist António Egas Moniz (1874–1955) began tests on human subjects. It may seem shocking to us today, but he won a Nobel Prize in 1949 for this controversial form of surgery.

NOW YOU SEE IT – BUT WHAT IS IT?

Callosotomy involves the cutting of the corpus callosum, *which connects the two hemispheres of the brain, resulting in so-called 'split-brain' patients. It is sometimes used to treat*

> *intractable epilepsy. In experiments with split-brain patients, Roger Sperry discovered that an item seen with the left eye only cannot be named. This is because the information from the left eye goes to the right side of the brain, but the left side of the brain is, for most people, used for speech control. With no connection between the two halves of the brain, the left side can't know what the right side has seen and so can't name it.*

Talking therapies

In contrast to the drastic physical treatments that emerged in the 20th century was the 'talking therapy', developed first by Sigmund Freud.

In his psychoanalytic method, diagnosis and treatment progress together. Talking at length with a psychoanalyst both uncovers the problem and, by enabling the patient to bring it out and examine it, reduces its negative impact and begins healing.

FREUD'S CONTRIBUTION

Freud developed the 'talking cure' into the full-blown psychoanalytic method, championed it, and is generally associated with it. His method has become part of the therapeutic repertoire, and still informs analysis techniques today.

From 1885–86, Freud studied in Paris with the great hypnotist Jean-Martin Charcot. Charcot believed that hysteria could be triggered, at least in part, by psychological causes. On his return from Paris, Freud began in private practice in Vienna, specializing in hysteria and using hypnosis. But he ran into problems. Some patients could not be hypnotized. Others refused to believe his interpretation of the 'recovered memories' they had revealed under hypnosis. He eventually tried another method. He had patients lie on a couch, close their eyes and recount their experiences of a symptom. He had developed the method known as free association and, by chance, the enduring icon of psychoanalysis – the analyst's couch.

THE CASE OF ANNA O.

The method of psychoanalysis originated with the treatment of 'Anna O.' (actually Bertha Pappenheim). Twenty-one years old, Anna had suffered a range of physical symptoms including partial paralysis, eating disorders, speech disturbances, disorientation and memory loss while and after caring for her father during his long, final illness. She was diagnosed with 'hysteria' and treated by Joseph Breuer (1842–1925), initially using hypnosis.

Each time Breuer got her to recall when she had first experienced a symptom, the symptom disappeared, at least temporarily. Breuer concluded that some ideas or memories were too painful to bear conscious scrutiny and instead were manifested as physical symptoms. When the suppressed energy of the distress was dissipated through talking about it, the correlating symptom was no longer needed, and vanished.

Breuer saw Anna O. for around 1,000 hours over 18 months. Although he considered her cured, she was to spend a considerable time in a mental institution and took large amounts of morphine for her continuing pain. Years later, as a successful social worker, she strongly resisted any suggestion that those in her care be psychoanalyzed.

Later researchers have often concluded that Anna O.'s problems were in fact neurological and therefore were never going to be cured by psychoanalysis. It was Anna O. who first coined the term 'talking cure'.

CONCLUSION
The riddle of the mind

The story of psychology is still very much under way – we are not far from the opening pages and have no idea how the story will end.

The mind/body problem, first fully articulated by Descartes, still lies at the heart of psychology, not only unresolved, but further complicated by the work of the intervening years. We could now speak of a mind/brain/body problem, or even a thinking/mind/brain/body problem. Just as the contents of a book are not the same as the physical object of the book, so the mind and its contents and functions are beginning to be prised apart. Cognitive scientists focusing on the algorithmic or computing model of the brain, and neurologists looking at its mechanics and chemistry, have helped to separate mental activity from the mind itself.

Our conception of the 'mind', after Freud, has to take account of unconscious as well as conscious mental activity. As we begin to look at the brain with electronic equipment, we find stunning results – such as the apparent making of a 'decision' before we are consciously aware of it. This throws into doubt the role of the conscious mind and the existence of free will.

IS FREE WILL AN ILLUSION?
Itzhak Fried, working in California and Tel Aviv, reported in 2011 that by monitoring an electrode implanted in the brain he could 'see' subjects making a decision to press a button a second-and-a-half before the subject believed they had decided. From the electrode information, Fried could predict with 80 per cent accuracy which choice the subject would make. Apparently, the 'decision' is made somehow in the unconscious mind and represented in the conscious mind as an act of free will, after it has already been determined.

Into the future

Today, psychiatry depends on a combination of drug treatments, talking therapies and, occasionally, some form of psychosurgery. By no means all patients can be helped. And it's still not really clear how we should define abnormal psychology and whether we can distinguish it.

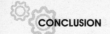

The one and the many

Each of the schools of psychological thought attempts to look in a particular way at why we are as we are and act as we do. But the schools are largely incompatible. Psychology has fragmented into myriad different approaches and studies, sometimes in conflict and sometimes simply coexisting.

A few psychologists, including Gregg Henriques of Vermont University, seek a 'unifying theory' for psychology that will bring it together. The standard model of the atom, general relativity and quantum mechanics provide a framework within which physics currently operates. Biology has evolution and genetics which, together, can account for the ways organisms work and develop. Psychology is without a frame of reference on which all practitioners agree and within which developments and ideas can be assessed and tested. Some psychologists say that such a unifying theory is not possible. The fundamental split between the behaviourist and mentalist schools means there is not even agreement on whether the mind exists, let alone how we might study and measure it in valid ways.

ON BEING SANE IN INSANE PLACES

In 1973, the American psychologist David Rosenhan (1929–2012) carried out an experiment with rather terrifying results. He sent eight healthy people (including himself) to psychiatric hospitals in the USA where they faked auditory hallucinations. All were admitted as patients. After admission, they acted normally and said they had no more hallucinations. The average time they spent in hospital was 19 days, and all had to admit to having a mental disorder and agree to taking antipsychotic drugs before they were allowed to leave.

All but one was diagnosed with 'schizophrenia in remission'. After an outcry from the psychiatric profession, Rosenhan accepted a challenge from one hospital to send imposters over a period of a year and they guaranteed they would recognize them. Over the course of the following year, of 193 new patients, 41 were identified as potential Rosenhan fakes. In fact, Rosenhan hadn't sent any patients at all. He concluded, 'It is clear that we cannot distinguish the sane from the insane in psychiatric hospitals.'

It's likely that as time passes an increasing amount will be discovered to link mental states and acts with neuroscience and brain chemistry. This might offer new ways of understanding and treating abnormal psychology. But it's unlikely that it will fully explain the mental state of being human – what it feels like to be in love, hear music, or engage in a creative act. We might never be able to say why any particular individual will prefer one political theory to another, believe in God or dislike sport. Noam Chomsky believes that some problems are beyond the capability of the human brain to comprehend. The nature of our own minds might fall into that category.

'My hunch . . . is that the answer to the riddle of free will lies in the domain of potential science that the human mind can never master because of the limitations of its genetic structure. . . . In principle, there are almost certainly true scientific theories that our genetically determined brain structures will prevent us from ever understanding.'

Noam Chomsky, 1983

Index

abnormal psychology
  and the brain 227–9
  classifications of 232–6
  early ideas of 219–26,
    232–3
  and Sigmund Freud
    229–32
  treatments for 236–49
Abu Ghraib 202–3
adaptive act 76
Adler, Alfred 41, 77,
  177–80, 230
Adrian, Edgar 55
Africanus, Joannes Leo 222
Agassiz, Louis 69
Akbar the Great 44
Alcmaeon of Croton 107
Allport, Gordon 136
American psychology 71–2
Anatomy of Melancholy, The
  (Burton) 226–7
Angell, James Rowland 75–6
'Anna O.' 248–9
Aquinas, Thomas 18, 25
archetypes 123–4
Aretaeus 233
Aristotle 8, 15, 16, 17, 19,
  20, 21, 168, 193
Arnauld, Antoine 132
Aronson, Elliot 191–2
Asch, Solomon 211, 212–13
Asclepiades of Bithynia 224,
  232, 239
associationism 112–17, 144
astrology 158–9
Atkinson, Richard 151
Atkinson–Shiffrin model of
  memory 151–2
attachment theory 182–7
Augustine of Hippo 18
Avicenna 19–20, 21–2, 24,
  125, 219–20
Bacon, Francis 22, 104
Bain, Alexander 142–3
Baldwin, James Mark 88
Bandura, Paul 205–6
Bartlett, Frederic 131,
  133–4, 149
Bedlam 242–3
behaviourism 11, 37, 85–92,
  94–6, 179–80
Behind the Shock Machine
  (Perry) 210
Bell, Charles 53–5
Bem, Daryl J. 192
Berkeley, George 13, 110–11
Bessel, Friedrich 55–6
Binet, Alfred 172, 174
Binet–Simon scale 172
Birney, Robert 137
blank slate (*tabula rasa*)
  124–7, 173

Bleuler, Paul Eugen 235
Bloom, Paul 204–5
Book of Travels (Çelebi)
  242–3
Bowlby, John 182–5
brain
  and abnormal psychology
    227–9
  and brain function
    99–100
  early ideas of 9, 16, 49
  elasticity of 100–1
  experiments on nerves
    49–55
  and mental functions 31
  and neurology 32
Brave New World (Huxley)
  87
Brentano, Franz 105
Breuer, Joseph 248
Broca, Paul Pierre 228
Burton, Richard 226–7
bystander effect 98–9,
  213–15
Cajal, Ramón y 154
callosotomy 246–7
Campanella, Tommaso 27
Canon of Medicine
  (Avicenna) 20, 21–2
Carlsmith, James Merrill 73,
  191–2
Carr, Harvey 76
Çelebi, Evliya 241, 242–3
Celsus, Aulus Cornelius
  233, 240
Charcot, Jean-Martin 35,
  170, 223, 247
Chiarugi, Vincenzo 243
child development 180–8
child prodigies 175–6
Chomsky, Noam 132, 253
cognitive behaviour therapy
  (CBT) 93
cognitive dissonance 190–2
cognitive psychology 11,
  97–8
cognitive science 30–1
*Common Sense Book of Baby
  and Child Care, The*
  (Spock) 187, 188
conditioning 139–46
conformity 207–17
criminality 167–8
Critique of Pure Reason
  (Kant) 129
Crooke, Helkiah 49–50
Darley, John 214
D'Arpentigny, Casimir
  Stanislas 169
Darwin, Charles 123, 164–5,
  197, 207
Darwin, William 207

De Anima (Aristotle) 8
De Medicina (Celsus) 233
Dead Sea Scrolls 20–1
Democritus 107
demonstrative knowledge
  103
Dennett, Daniel 31
depression 226–7
Descartes, René 22–6, 50–1,
  104, 121
determinism 157–8
developmental stages 130–1,
  136–7, 150–1
Dewey, John 75, 149, 150
Dias, Brian 198
*Diagnostic and Statistical
  Manual* (DSM) 235–6
Dickens, Charles 167–8
Dix, Dorothea 243
Donders, Franciscus 61–2
Ehrenfels, Christian von 79
Eichmann, Adolf 212, 216
Einstein, Albert 40–1
electroconvulsive therapy
  (ECT) 245–6
Elements of Psychophysics
  (Fechner) 60
emergence 84
Émile (Rousseau) 150
empirical knowledge 103
empiricism 103–4
Enlightenment, The 22, 23
Epictetus 17
Epicurus 16, 108
epilepsy 220–1, 225
Esquirol, Jean-Etienne 244
*Essay Concerning Human
  Understanding, An*
  (Locke) 109, 120, 126,
  127
Essay on Man (Pope) 7
evolution 69–70
experimental psychology
  43–8
Fabre, Jean-Henri Casimir
  137
Fallon, James 230
Fechner, Gustav 58–60, 110,
  112, 124
Feigl, Herbert 93
Feldman, Heidi 133
feral children 46–7
Festinger, Leon 73, 190–1,
  192
'forbidden experiment' 43–4,
  121, 132
Frederick II 43–4
free will 72–3, 157–8, 251
Freud, Ann 230
Freud, Sigmund 10–11,
  33–6, 40–1, 76–7, 138,
  174–5, 177, 199, 223,